THE SECRET
IN
LALITA SAHASRANAMA

Seek the transformative potential enshrined
within Lalita Sahasranama
(Law of Attraction and Chakra Meditation)

Authored by:
DEEPIKA ARORA

Well-founded in the Self, Lalita is a free consciousness that radiates the Self's joyful and vibrant essence

śrīmahātripurasundarīṃ śrīvidyāṃ śrīlalitāmbikāṃ
kāmeśīṃ parameśvarīṃ śrīcakreśvarīṃ namāmi

I bow to the Supreme Goddess, the beauty of the three worlds, the source of all knowledge, the auspicious Lalita, the one who fulfills desires, the supreme ruler, the queen of the Sri Chakra

This book is dedicated to you

ACKNOWLEDGEMENTS

This book wouldn't have come to fruition without the profound influence of the Divine Source, the ultimate source of inspiration and creativity. My heartfelt gratitude goes to this ever-present force for guiding me on this journey.

Additionally, I am immensely grateful to my family and well-wishers, their unwavering support and love provided a constant source of strength and encouragement throughout the writing process. Their presence has been a true blessing.

CONTENTS

This book embarks on a journey to unveil the profound connections between self-empowerment, spiritual practices, and the ancient wisdom of Lalita Sahasranama.

This chapter explores the fundamental principles of the Law of Attraction and introduces a powerful breathing technique to amplify its effects.

This chapter delves into the fascinating connection between the Law of Attraction and the relevant verses of Lalita Sahasranama, exploring how both principles encourage mindful manifestation.

This chapter explores the concepts of spiritual healing and chakra meditation, focusing specifically on verses 38-40 of Lalita Sahasranama and their role in fostering inner well-being.

This chapter unveils the secrets of chakra meditation, providing a step-by-step guide to activate energy centers for holistic healing.

This chapter introduces the practice of Sri Yantra Meditation, also known as Sri Yantra Tratak, and explains its benefits for enhancing focus and spiritual growth.

This final chapter presents the complete Lalita Sahasranama for chanting, aiming to unlock its profound wisdom and power.

Lalita Devi: Unveiling the Divine Within
Sri Yantra and the Human Connection
Verses on the Battlefield
The Story of Sati and Daksha
Six Paths of Devotion

ABOUT THE BOOK

The popularity of Law of Attraction and Spiritual Healing books raises the question: Is the Law of Attraction and Spiritual Healing real? The concept gained traction in recent years with books like "The Secret" and "The Power of Subconscious Mind" but does it truly hold the power to bring good fortune? However, I found that I was still disconnected from these simplified concepts.

This feeling of disconnect motivated me to research the original spiritual sources, leading me to conclude that the Law of Attraction's true essence isn't the simple "Ask, Believe, Receive" formula. Instead, the core principle is "Alignment," which requires a conscious raising of one's vibrational energy.

For 21 years, my life lacked direction. Due to personal circumstances, I started a journey in meditation two years ago. Despite having various skills, I struggled to achieve success in any field. Aspiring to leave mediocrity behind, I, an "Average Joe," started seeking ways to become a "Successful Moe."

Living in South India, I was drawn to the famous Lalita Sahasranama chant. One day, I stumbled upon a Law of Attraction video by motivational speaker Sneh Desai, picked up Rhonda Byrne's "The Secret" and delved into information about Sri Vidya, Mahavidyas, and the Law of Attraction.

Putting Law of Attraction principles into practice, I observed my desires aligning with my mindset. This experience solidified my belief that "everything is in our mind" and our "emotional state decides everything." Additionally, I held faith in the power of Lalita Sahasranama, which is said to transform destiny, burn karmas, and dispel negativity. However, I questioned how chanting could dissolve karmas.

To further my understanding, I researched on Kundali (astrological charts) and Chakras. This exploration completely changed my perspective on Kundali. It's important to note that chanting Lalita Sahasranama alone does not guarantee life changes. One must understand its significance and practice it with gratitude, as gratitude is known to have high vibrations. Similarly, the Law of Attraction requires adherence to specific principles if one wants to manifest consciously.

Fueled by a desire for answers, I embarked on a journey filled with sleepless nights and vivid dreams. I eventually concluded that "We are miniatures of the universe" and where we focus our attention is what we attract. This solidified my belief that the Law of Attraction is not a scam and challenged the limiting beliefs instilled in me from childhood.

To deepen my knowledge, I delved into books by renowned authors like Rhonda Byrne, Joseph Murphy, and V. Ravi. It was a long journey filled with distractions, but I gleaned valuable information from their books. Spending time with children, who naturally possess high vibrations, further aided my learning.

One day, while sleeping, inspiration struck – to decode the Lalita Sahasranama in my way. I decided to capture my understanding on paper rather than letting it remain in my wandering mind. Beyond simply chanting the 1000 names, I began to see it as a way of life, shifting from chanting individual names to verses. Sri Satya Narayana Sarma's book, YouTube videos from Sri Vidya Masters, and the guidance of Sri V. Ravi (founder of www.manblunder.com) and Sri Sumit Sharma from Haridwar further enriched my journey. I also participated in live Lalita Sahasranama sessions led by Sri Vidya Master Smt. Smita Venkatesh.

Sri Ravi Ji, once said the following words: "It's all in your mind. You can change your life by following simple breathing techniques (breath control) and focusing on your desires, even without mantras" resonated deeply. I held onto these words, realizing the universe was offering knowledge and marking the end of my search in this direction. That day, I decided to move forward in life, and many of my limiting beliefs began to fade, although some remain embedded in my subconscious. This book also provides a secret breathing technique for manifestation. The source of that breathing technique can also be found in Shiv Swarodya and Vijnana Bhairav Tantra.

Driven by the vision I had during my Sri Vidya Sadhana journey, where I envisioned decoding the Lalita Sahasranama, and the belief that everyone has their spiritual path, I decided to share my interpretation based on Advaita philosophy (God and I are not different) and understanding of interconnectedness. While acknowledging the time constraints of busy lives, I have chosen to comment on selected verses and have provided the full 183 verses for chanting at the end for those who wish to delve deeper. To enhance reader comprehension, the chapter outlining the Law of Attraction principles, universal laws and process precedes the chapter on relevant verses. This structure allows readers to grasp the concept before delving into supporting scriptural references.

In conclusion, I intend to emphasize that the Law of Attraction and Spiritual Healing have always existed and are timeless. Sri Vidya is considered the highest form of spiritual guidance available. Lalita Sahasranama is an important aspect of Sri Vidya. Lalita Sahasranama holds countless secrets, and exploring them could take a lifetime.

To avoid overwhelming readers, I initially focused on explaining the most relevant verses on Law of Attraction and then three verses on Chakra Meditation. Understanding these explained verses would equip you to grasp the others. To encourage deeper reflection, the book includes a section of thought-provoking prompts at its close.

Lalita Sahasranama is said to encompass the knowledge of all Vedas and Upanishads. By starting your chant slowly and consistently, the hidden meanings within may gradually unfold. Remember, Shiv-Shakti, the divine union, serves as the ultimate teacher.

Best of luck on your journey. May Devi Maa bless you with both material and spiritual abundance.

INTRODUCTION TO LALITA SAHASRANAMA

Sri Vidya: Unveiling the Divine Light Within

Sri Vidya is a profound spiritual path that unlocks the secrets of the universe. It delves into the nature of the supreme energy (Sri) and the hidden reality (Tattva) behind the physical world (Prakriti). This knowledge encompasses the processes of creation, sustenance, and dissolution. It also illuminates the divine consciousness (Chaitanya) and its essence (Tattva). It aims to reveal the fundamental nature of reality and the inherent divinity residing within each individual.

Pure Knowledge, Not Ritual

Unlike some tantric practices, Sri Vidya emphasizes pure knowledge (Shuddha Vidya) rather than external rituals. The term "Sri" transcends gender, signifying a universal truth, not a female concept (Stri Vidya). Sri Vidya is an internal exploration, similar to Yoga, requiring no material objects.

The Inner Light of Chaitanya

"Chaitanya" is a Sanskrit word which means supreme consciousness, supreme knowledge, or supreme light. It is the fundamental reality that is the basis of all existence. It is often considered the inherent energy or principle that makes the universe alive and dynamic. It is not a physical object, but rather a pervasive, imperishable, and immutable truth. This Chaitanya does not come from an external source, but naturally resides within every living being. Just as sunlight pervades everywhere, similarly, Chaitanya is inherent in every soul. It is the core of our consciousness, the power that enables us to think, feel, and experience.

This inner light manifests uniquely to different people, appearing as Ganesha, Krishna, Shiva, Devi, or other divine forms, depending on their inclinations. This internal manifestation is a personalized experience of the same universal Chaitanya.

Lalita Sahasranama: A Treasure Trove

Lalita Sahasranama, a sacred text, holds immense importance in Sri Vidya. It encapsulates the entire essence of this spiritual path. Encoded within it are profound secrets about the universe and creation. This text is considered a treasure trove of incredible knowledge.

Authorship Attributed to the Divine

The authorship of Lalita Sahasranama is not attributed to a single human. As the Brahmanda Purana tells us, the eight goddesses of speech (Vaag Devis) composed it under the guidance of the goddess Lalita Devi herself. These eight goddesses are Vasini, Kameshwari, Aruna, Vimala, Jayani, Modini, Sarveshvari, and Kaulini. Lalita Sahasranama finds application in various forms of worship, including recitation (Parayana), offering (Archana), and fire rituals (Homa). This powerful stotram is believed to have been revealed during a discourse between Lord Hayagriva and the sage Agastya.

Beyond the Statue

Murti puja, or statue worship in Hinduism, is a practice that helps individuals connect with the divine. While the statue itself is a physical object, it symbolizes a deeper spiritual reality. It's not the material that is worshipped, but the divine essence it represents. The statue acts as a focal point for contemplation and a channel for divine energy. Hinduism recognizes that the ultimate reality (Brahman) is formless and infinite, thus the diverse array of deities and images allows individuals to connect with the divine in a way that resonates with them personally. This fosters tolerance and acceptance of different paths to the same ultimate truth. Images serve as a bridge to the infinite, a "veil" that makes the divine accessible to our senses, eventually leading to inner worship.

Masculine and Feminine Energy

In Lalita Sahasranama, Shiva and Shakti are fundamental, representing two complementary and inseparable aspects of reality. They are often described as the masculine and feminine principles, but this is symbolic, not literal.

Shiva represents the static, unchanging aspect of the universe - pure consciousness, the potential for creation. He is often depicted as a meditating ascetic, symbolizing detachment and transcendence. Think of him as the unmanifested potential, the seed of the universe.

Shakti, on the other hand, embodies the dynamic, active force - energy, power, and manifestation. She is the life force, the power that brings Shiva's potential into being. She is the mother of the universe, the source of all creation, movement, and change.

It's crucial to understand that this is not about traditional gender roles. Both Shiva and Shakti reside within every individual, regardless of their biological sex or gender identity. These principles represent the interplay of consciousness and energy within us all.

Their union is essential. Just as consciousness without energy is inert, energy without consciousness is chaotic. The dance of Shiva and Shakti gives rise to the entire universe. This union is sometimes represented by the Ardhanarishvara, a deity depicted as half male and half female, symbolizing the unity of these two forces.

In essence, the Shiva-Shakti is a powerful metaphor for the interconnectedness of all things. It highlights the balance between stillness and action, potential and manifestation, which are necessary for a complete and fulfilling life. Understanding these principles can lead to a deeper understanding of ourselves and our place in the cosmos.

Chapter 1
Mastering Manifestation: Understanding the Law of Attraction Process

❋

This chapter breaks down the core principles of the Law of Attraction, universal laws offering practical insights into harnessing its potential for conscious manifestation.

The Law of Attraction is a belief system suggesting a connection between our thoughts and feelings and what we experience in life. It proposes that positive thoughts and emotions tend to lead to positive outcomes, while negative ones tend to attract negative experiences. This connection is often described as a form of attraction, like a magnet drawing similar energies.

This philosophy emphasizes the importance of cultivating a positive mindset to attract desired results in various aspects of life, including health, finances, and relationships. However, it's important to understand that the Law of Attraction is not a scientifically proven law, but rather a personal development philosophy. The Law of Attraction is built upon these core principles:

Everything is Energy: The Law of Attraction philosophy aligns with the fundamental principle - Everything is energy, vibrating at its own frequency. Everything in the universe, from the food we consume to the stars, is ultimately composed of energy in various forms. **(The Law of Vibration)**

Energy and You: We are more than just physical; we are energetic beings, all connected by a common origin. Our thoughts and emotions each vibrate at a unique frequency. We hold incredible potential and the capacity for remarkable growth. By exploring the interconnectedness of our minds, bodies, and the world around us, we gain a deeper understanding of ourselves and unlock a vast wellspring of abilities. We are not isolated but integral parts of a vast cosmic network, interconnected with everything – humans, animals, plants, and even minerals – through an invisible web of energy and consciousness. This energy field is the source of infinite creativity and pure knowledge. Our actions, thoughts, and emotions have ripple effects throughout this interconnected reality. This newfound awareness empowers us to not only enrich our own lives but also contribute meaningfully to the betterment of humanity. **(The Law of Divine Oneness and The Law of Pure Potentiality)**

Like attracts like: The idea behind this principle is that our thoughts and experiences are linked. It suggests that focusing on the positive – both in thoughts and feelings – can lead to more positive results in life. On the other hand, negativity tends to attract negative experiences. Some explain this as a kind of **"mirror effect"** where our inner state reflects and attracts similar energy from the world around us. This is often explained as a form of **"resonance"**, where our internal state attracts similar energies from the outside world. The Law of Attraction emphasizes that our focus determines what we attract. While desire is the starting point, it must be coupled with positive intention. Consistently focusing on our goals through thought, discussion, visualization, and feeling increases the likelihood of attracting them, provided they are aligned with good intentions. Our environment also significantly influences our thoughts and feelings, impacting what we attract. Ultimately, we attract what we are. Our inner world, made up of our traits, convictions, and deeds, has a way of attracting similar experiences, people, and situations into our lives. **(The Law of Intention & Desire)**

Self-Love and Self-Referral: The Foundation for Attraction - True self-love involves accepting yourself fully, even your flaws. It also means recognizing your unlimited potential for growth and achievement. Within the Law of Attraction, self-love is crucial because it cultivates a positive internal state that attracts favorable experiences. To strengthen self-love, learn to quiet the negative opinions of others and prioritize your own well-being. For this, we must connect with our true-self. It requires to reach the state of self-referral. Self-awareness, or "self-referral," centers our focus on our inner being, our soul, rather than external factors. The alternative, "object-referral," means we're constantly swayed by external influences like situations, people, and possessions. In this state, our ego, our self-constructed image or social mask, becomes our primary reference point. Driven by a need for approval and control, and fucled by underlying fear, the ego constantly seeks validation and power. Our authentic self, our soul, exists beyond such limitations. It's untouched by criticism, unafraid of any obstacle, and feels inherently equal to all. This inherent equality fosters both humility and a lack of superiority, as it recognizes the shared essence of Self, the same unique spark of life animating every individual.

Authentic self-knowledge unlocks our full potential. We realize that the same life energy flows through us all, and is the true basis of what we perceive as material wealth. This realization dispels fear and insecurity. We understand that past mistakes, anger, and hatred arose from a lack of self-awareness and the mistaken belief that happiness comes from external objects. This realization leads to bliss, fostering stillness, a practice of silence, and the cessation of judgment. We develop a deep love for us, nature and all beings, cultivating inner stability. Because our inner state reflects our outer world, we begin to experience abundance in all aspects of our lives. **(The Law of Pure Potentiality)**

Embrace the Present Moment: This principle emphasizes the importance of focusing on the present moment rather than dwelling on the past or worrying about the future. While some situations may seem challenging, the Law of Attraction encourages focusing on what you can control and taking action to improve the here and now. Instead of feeling overwhelmed or unhappy, it suggests channeling your energy into finding ways to make your present moment the best it can be. This proactive approach allows you to create a positive foundation for future experiences.

Manifesting your desires requires a two-pronged approach: relinquishing control and trusting the timing. Let go of any need to micromanage or obsess over the outcome, trusting that the universe has received your request and is actively working on it. Simultaneously, cultivate patience and trust in the universe's timeline. Avoid discouragement if progress seems slow; the universe may be working in unseen ways to orchestrate the perfect unfolding of your goals. Detachment from the outcome is key. Clinging to a specific result breeds insecurity and fear, which lowers your vibrational frequency and can ultimately hinder the manifestation process. Act as if your wish has already been granted. **(The Law of Detachment and The Law of Assumption)**

Release Negativity for Positive Attraction: The Law of Attraction posits that negative emotions like fear, jealousy, anger, revenge and greed can obstruct the flow of positive experiences. To attract what you desire, it's important to cultivate positive emotions and a sense of abundance. Instead of indulging in negativity or gossip, celebrate the successes of others. Recognize that there is enough for everyone and actively tap into that abundance with desire, knowledge, and action. Let go of complaining and negativity, and replace them with gratitude. Remember, shifting your mindset takes time and practice. Stay away from negative influences and focus on cultivating positivity for the best results. Avoid coveting or holding onto what belongs to others. You possess the potential to achieve anything you desire. Generously serve both people and nature, understanding that the Law of Karma applies universally - "What goes around comes around." **(The Law of Karma and The Law of Compensation)**

Embrace Forgiveness for Progress: The Law of Attraction emphasizes the importance of forgiveness, both for ourselves and others. We all make mistakes, and holding onto anger or guilt hinders our ability to move forward and attract positive experiences. Forgiveness allows you to release negative emotions and create space for positive energy to flow. By letting go of past hurts and resentments, you open yourself up to new possibilities and attract more joyful experiences in your life. True repentance opens the door to universal forgiveness, but that door swings both ways. Forgiving others is essential to receiving it yourself. **(The Law of Karma and The Law of Compensation)**

Shed Limiting Beliefs, Embrace Abundance: The Law of Attraction highlights the importance of recognizing and overcoming limiting beliefs that can create obstacles to attracting what you desire. If you believe in scarcity, you will subconsciously attract circumstances that reflect that belief. Instead, embrace the concept of abundance – the understanding that there is enough for everyone. Wealthy individuals often embody the abundance mindset, believing in limitless possibilities. Recognize that there is no virtue in poverty. We all need and deserve financial well-being to live fulfilling lives. Release any limiting beliefs that may prevent you from actively attracting prosperity. **(The Law of Abundance)**

The Power of Faith and Positive Thinking: Cultivating unshakeable faith is essential when working with the Law of Attraction. This means trusting in the process and believing in the power of the universe, even when doubts may arise. Release negative opinions, both from yourself and others, as they can hinder progress. Believe in a greater force that responds to your dominant thoughts and feelings. Remember, emotions and thoughts act as magnets, attracting experiences that mirror their energy. Reflect on your life – you'll likely see examples where both fear and doubt, as well as confidence and positivity, have manifested in your life. This reinforces that the Law of Attraction is always at work. Embrace the possibility of achieving your desires. Replace negativity with positive expectations, and you'll begin attracting more favorable experiences into your life. Our thoughts possess immense power to manifest reality and influence our vibrational frequency. **(The Law of Vibration)**

Inspired Action: Inspired action is the vital link transforming desires into tangible results. While the Law of Attraction highlights the power of visualizing desired outcomes, inspired action provides the "how" – the active steps to realization, often requiring us to step out of our comfort zone. This involves a deliberate approach to learn, plan, and act decisively. This isn't about strained effort but about taking action prompted by intuition, inner knowing, or a sense of purpose. This aligned action feels natural and energizing, often unlocking unexpected opportunities and synchronicities – the effortless action stemming from inspiration and alignment. **(The Law of Inspired Action and The Law of Least Effort)**

Cultivate Gratitude and Practice Giving for Abundance: The Law of Attraction emphasizes the power of gratitude in attracting positive experiences. By expressing sincere appreciation for what you already have, big or small, you signal to the universe that you are open to receiving more abundance. Gratitude shifts your focus from lack to appreciation, raising your vibrational energy – a key element in the Law of Attraction. Saying "thank you" with genuine feeling is said to have a particularly high vibrational frequency, fostering an abundance mindset. Expressing gratitude not only to the universe but also to those who have helped you along the way reinforces positive connections and attracts supportive individuals. As you cultivate an attitude of gratitude, you open yourself up to receiving more blessings in life.

Energy and prosperity depend on a constant flow. Just as a river needs to move to thrive, so do we. The Universe operates through giving and receiving. The more we give, the more we receive, keeping abundance circulating. Value multiplies when shared. The Law of Giving is simple: give what you want. Want joy? Give it. Love? Give it. Appreciation? Give it. Material abundance? Help others achieve it. Helping others is the best way to help ourselves. And the most powerful gifts are often non-material: care, attention, affection, appreciation, and love. Our giving should be without expectation of return. We are inherently abundant because nature generously provides for our needs and desires. **(The Law of Abundance and The Law of Giving & Receiving)**

Important Considerations:

The Law of Attraction is not without its critics, particularly regarding potential misinterpretations. Here are some key points to consider:

Avoid Self-Blame: Critics raise concerns that the Law of Attraction can lead to self - blame for uncontrollable events like accidents or illnesses. While focusing on a positive outlook can be beneficial, it's crucial to remember that not all circumstances are within our control.

Focus on Response: The Law of Attraction emphasizes focusing on our responses to challenges, rather than dwelling on the challenges themselves. Difficult situations can hold unforeseen opportunities, and our resilient response can be a source of strength and growth.

Healthy Balance: It's essential to maintain a healthy balance between positive thinking and taking responsibility for our actions. The Law of Attraction doesn't replace accountability or excuse negative behavior.

Seeking Help: If you're struggling with mental or physical health challenges, the Law of Attraction is not a substitute for professional help. Always seek guidance from qualified professionals when needed.

By understanding these limitations and utilizing the Law of Attraction with awareness, it can be a helpful tool for fostering a positive outlook and promoting personal growth. Remember, it's important to maintain healthy perspectives and seek professional help when necessary.

MANIFESTING WITH THE LAW OF ATTRACTION: A STEP-BY-STEP GUIDE

STEP 1:

Find Your Calm Center

The first step to manifestation is finding your calm center. This means quieting internal and external distractions to connect with your inner self.

Here are some suggestions for achieving relaxation:

Meditate: Dedicate 10-15 minutes to meditation. This practice helps quiet the mind, allowing you to think clearly and release negative self-talk. I recommend Chakra Meditation, it is a helpful tool to overcome even past traumas.

Pranayama Breathing: Consider incorporating Pranayama breathing techniques into your meditation practice. These specific breathing exercises can further promote calmness and clarity.

Silence the Inner Chatter: Through meditation and breathing exercises, you can quiet the negative voices in your head and gain control over your thoughts. Don't try to suppress the inner chatter. Just acknowlege and do some breathing exercises like Alternative Nose Breathing or just focus on inahalation and exhalation of breath. A calm mind allows you to think clearly about your desires. This clarity helps you visualize your goals and direct your energy towards achieving them.

Sri Yantra Tratak: This specific meditation technique, which may be explored later in the book, can also be a helpful tool for finding relaxation.

Remember: Relaxation is the foundation for effective manifestation. By quieting your mind and clearing distractions, you can set the stage for setting intentions, visualizing desires and taking action towards your dreams.

After achieving a state of relaxation, the next step is to clarify your desires. Remember, the Law of Attraction is limited only by your imagination.

STEP 2:

Ask with Clarity and Feeling

With a calm mind, it's time to define your desires – this is the essence of "asking" within the Law of Attraction. Remember, the possibilities are limitless, guided only by your imagination.

Define Your Vision: Imagine your ideal life: Where are you? Who are you with? What experiences fill your days? Be specific and detailed in your vision.

Identify Your Desires: What do you truly want to experience, acquire, or become? Be clear on your desires, both big and small. Avoid sending mixed signals to the universe – unwavering clarity is crucial.

Make a Clear Request: Asking the universe is like placing an order: Be precise and confident in your request. Trust that the universe has "heard" your desires.

Feel the Feeling: Visualization alone isn't enough: Combine it with strong emotional connection. Imagine yourself experiencing what you desire, and embody the positive emotions associated with it. Some individuals struggle with visualization, that's perfectly OK, just imagine, but feeling is vital for sending the signal to the universe.

Create a Vision Board (Optional): Visually represent your desires: Create a vision board (collage) that combines images and words that embody your goals.

Be the Feeling: The universe responds to your energy: More than just asking, embody the emotions associated with achieving your desires. This powerful signal communicates your request clearly to the universe.

It's important to remember that feeling is a crucial aspect of the Law of Attraction, often overlooked by many. By combining clear vision/imagination with strong emotions, you communicate your desires effectively and create a powerful force for attracting them into your life.

Discover the Ultimate Manifestation Technique

Many follow manifestation techniques without seeing results. While making a wish, inhale deeply, hold your breath, state your desire, then exhale. Remember, never ask while exhaling. Our breath is more than just a life sign; it influences our internal processes and external experiences.

Important Considerations:

Shift Your Focus to What You Desire

The Law of Attraction emphasizes the power of focusing on what you want to attract, rather than what you don't want. This is because:

Negative phrasing carries negative energy: Sentences like "I don't want to be sad" still hold the emotional energy of sadness. The universe is believed to respond to the underlying energy, not just the words.

The universe understands positive affirmations: Instead of negating something unwanted, clearly state your desired outcome: "I am happy" carries positive energy and clearly communicates your desire.

Focus on the goal, not the obstacle: Phrases like "I don't want to be late" keep your attention on the negative outcome of being late. Instead, shift your focus to the desired outcome: "I want to reach early."

Express desires clearly and positively: Avoid using "if" or "but" in your affirmations. Be clear, concise, and positive in expressing your desires.

Never ask for what is unethical or can harm others. It would come back to you with double force.

By reframing your desires in this way, you can leverage the Law of Attraction more effectively. Remember, the universe is said to respond to the energy you put out, so focus on the positive and watch your desires unfold.

Forget about the competition! Law of Attraction is all about your energy. It doesn't care how many other people want the same thing. Focus on what you desire and visualize it clearly. Believe in your ability to create your reality, and let go of fear. With positive thoughts and unwavering belief, you can attract what you want.

STEP 3:

Believe and Trust the Process

Cultivate Belief: The Law of Attraction emphasizes the importance of believing in the power of your thoughts. This means truly believing that your desires have the potential to manifest. Remember, if you haven't thought of something, it wouldn't be a possibility for you.

Trust the Universe: Have complete faith that the universe has received your request. When you ask with clarity and feeling, trust that the universe is working to bring your desires to fruition.

Patience and Gratitude: Be patient as your desires may not manifest immediately. The universe might have a different timeline, and your desires may even come in a better or more evolved form than initially envisioned. Let go of how things unfold, focusing on trust and gratitude. Express gratitude as if your desires have already manifested, reinforcing a positive and receptive state.

Overcoming Doubts: To strengthen your belief, consider using visualization or imagination and affirmations. Visualization/Imagination: Imagine yourself experiencing your desired outcome in vivid detail, engaging all your senses. This can trick your subconscious mind into believing it's real and pave the way for manifestation. Affirmations: Repeat positive statements about achieving your desires, gradually replacing doubts with unwavering belief.

Remember: The Law of Attraction is a journey. Cultivating strong belief, trust, and patience is essential for attracting your desires. Engage in practices like visualization/imagination and affirmations to support your journey and witness the power of positive thought and belief.

STEP 4:

Knowledge & Action

The Law of Attraction emphasizes the importance of knowledge and action alongside positive thinking and clear intention. Here's how:

Recognize Opportunities: The universe may present opportunities that can help you move closer to your desires. These can be unexpected events, helpful people, or insights that guide you forward. Be open and receptive to recognizing them when they arise.

Align Effort with Desire: Taking smart and dedicated action is crucial. While the universe may guide and support you, it's not a substitute for hard work. Your effort and initiative demonstrate your commitment to your goals and align your actions with your desires.

Trust Your Intuition: The best guide often lies within. Trust your intuition and inner knowing to discern the opportunities that resonate with you and your goals.

Step Out of Comfort Zone, Learn, Plan, and Act Decisively: Venture beyond your comfort zone and explore available resources to actively gain knowledge. This learning empowers you to develop a strategic action plan and, fueled by a positive mindset and strong beliefs, to embrace inspired action by courageously stepping outside your familiar routines, guiding your decisions.

Combine Dreaming with Doing: While dreaming and planning are important, don't let them become an excuse for inaction. Balance dreaming with concrete steps, turning your aspirations into a tangible plan and taking inspired action to make them a reality.

Remember: The Law of Attraction encourages a proactive approach to your dreams. By aligning belief, action, and intuition, you create fertile ground for your desires to manifest.

STEP 5:

Empower Yourself to Receive

Cultivate a Receiving Mindset: The final step in manifestation involves actively welcoming your desires. Feel the positive emotions associated with having your desires fulfilled. Imagine the joy, satisfaction, and gratitude you would experience if your wishes manifested.

Align Your Vibration: By feeling good, you raise your vibrational frequency, making you more receptive to attracting your desires. This aligns your inner state with the energy of your goals.

Trust the Process: Remember, the universe may have a bigger plan for you, sometimes offering something even better than what you initially requested. Trust the process and remain open to receiving what is ultimately in your highest good.

Express Gratitude: Feel gratitude for the blessings you already have and those yet to come. This reinforces positive energy flow and opens you up to receiving even more abundance.

Maintain a Positive Outlook: Don't dwell on doubts or anxieties. Focus on maintaining a positive mindset to remain receptive to what you desire.

Remember: Receiving is an active process, involving aligning your inner state with your desires and feeling worthy of them. By cultivating a receiving mindset, expressing gratitude, and maintaining a positive outlook, you create the space for your desires to manifest in your life

STEP 6:

Embrace Gratitude and Giving

The Law of Attraction highlights the importance of gratitude not only after receiving your desires but also throughout the manifestation process.

Practice Gratitude Regularly: Expressing gratitude as if you have already received your desires and also for your current blessings reinforces a positive and receptive state. This aligns your vibrational frequency with your goals and attracts them more readily.

Combine Gratitude and Unconditional Giving: When we combine gratitude and unconditional giving, we create a powerful synergy that can transform our lives and the lives of others. By giving from a place of gratitude, we amplify the positive energy of both actions. We should give freely and generously, appreciating the opportunity to make a difference in someone's life.

Gratitude Journal: Maintaining a gratitude journal is a powerful tool. Regularly reflecting on the blessings you already have cultivates an attitude of appreciation and reinforces a positive outlook.

The Power of Gratitude: Gratitude is not just about feeling good - it has the potential to:

Shift your mindset: By focusing on what you appreciate, you move away from negativity and attract positive experiences.

Raise your vibrational state: Gratitude elevates your energy, making you more receptive to your desires.

Improve various aspects of life: From health and relationships to financial well-being and happiness, gratitude can positively impact various aspects of your life.

Spark positive change: Practicing gratitude and giving unconditionally are two powerful principles that can significantly enhance our lives.

Remember: Gratitude is a powerful tool that can significantly enhance your experience with the Law of Attraction. By expressing appreciation for what you have and your future desires, you create a fertile ground for attracting positive experiences and manifesting your goals. Gratitude plays a significant role in harnessing the power of Lalita Sahasranama. By expressing gratitude, we acknowledge the blessings already present in our lives, attracting more abundance and positivity. Several names of the goddess within the chant embody abundance, prosperity, and wealth. Reciting them with a grateful heart attracts these positive energies into our lives. Shifting our focus from lack to abundance through gratitude allows us to manifest our desires more effectively. Gratitude practices, such as keeping a gratitude journal or expressing appreciation to others, can further amplify the manifestation process.

In conclusion, Lalita Sahasranama offers a powerful and multifaceted path to personal growth and well-being. When combined with the practice of gratitude, it becomes a potent tool for attracting positivity and manifesting your desires.

Please note: Though I have mentioned of chanting of Lalita Sahasranama, one can chant any mantra of God or give gratitude to universe or whomever one believes as God is One.

- 31 -

Important to Note

Release Control: It's crucial to avoid obsessing or micromanaging the outcome of your desires. Trust that the universe has received your request and is working towards its fulfillment. Let go of the need to control, and allow things to unfold organically.

Trust the Timing: Remember, the universe may have a different timeline for manifesting your desires. Trust the process and avoid getting discouraged by seemingly slow progress. The universe might be working behind the scenes, orchestrating events that will ultimately lead to your goals.

Embrace Openness: Be open to receiving your desires in unexpected ways. The universe may surprise you with opportunities or answers that differ from your initial expectations. Embrace flexibility and trust that even unexpected paths can lead to your desired outcome.

Grab Opportunities: While it's important to trust the universe, don't become passive. When opportunities arise that align with your goals, take action and seize them.

Analogy of Ordering: Think of asking the universe as placing an order from a menu. Trust that the restaurant (universe) has received your request, and they will prepare it with care. Focus on enjoying the waiting experience, knowing your order is on its way.

Remember: Letting go and trusting the process is a crucial aspect of the Law of Attraction. It allows you to release unnecessary anxieties and opens you up to receiving your desires in unexpected and fulfilling ways.

WATER MANIFESTATION TECHNIQUE

Want to turn your wishes into reality? Try the water manifestation technique!

This method, inspired by the law of attraction, uses water to amplify your desires. Believers say water absorbs energy, making it a perfect tool.

Here's how it works

Pick your vessel: Choose a dedicated glass or bottle. Avoid Steel vessel.

Get clear on your wish: What do you crave? A new job, love, or simply feeling grateful?

Infuse the water: Deeply Breathe In. As you pour, imagine your desire filling the water with positive energy, bringing you closer to your goal. Breathe Out.

Energize it further: Breathe In and hold the breath. Hold the container, focusing on the water. Imagine a bright light surrounding it, charging it with positivity. You can even say affirmations that match your goal. Breathe out.

Drink and believe: Consume the water or sprinkle it on yourself, truly believing it carries the energy of your wish. Feel it nourishing your body and aligning you with your dream.

Give thanks: Thank the universe for making your wish come true, even if it hasn't happened yet. Let go of attachment and trust the timing of the universe.

Repeat for best results: Do this daily, weekly, or whenever you feel drawn to it. Consistency and belief are key!

Important to Remember

People find that this technique helps them focus on goals and cultivate a positive mindset.

This practice works alongside taking action towards your dreams, not instead of it.

This technique is secretly mentioned in Phala Sruthi (The Fruits of Listening) of Lalita Sahasranama in the following verse:

Jalam-saṁ-mantrya-kumbhastham-nāma-sāhasrato mune,
Abhiṣhiñcheda-graha-grastān-grahā-naśhyantī-tat-kṣhanāt.

Which means Storing the water in a pot, and chanting the thousand names, oh sage, And anointing oneself with that water would remove all problems created by planets.

Please note: Though this verse mention of chanting of 1000 names, one can give gratitude by chanting mantra of God or to the universe or whomever one believes as God is One. This verse is taken from Lalita Sahasranama, so it mentions the chanting of 1000 names.

THE ULTIMATE BREATHING TECHNIQUE FOR MANIFESTING YOUR DESIRES - THE HIDDEN SECRET REVEALED

I am your breath, your life's very core.
Yet, unvalued, I'm often ignored.
When I depart, you'll feel the pain,
Realizing then, I was your domain.
You've taken me for granted, it's true,
But I'm more powerful than you.
Ask, and I'll give, all that you desire,
Acknowledge my essence, and soar to new heights.

We are microcosms of the universe, reflecting the external world within ourselves. Our subconscious mind, a powerful force, can be reprogrammed through various techniques, including breathwork. Swara Yoga, the Tantric Science of Brain Breathing, is one such powerful tool.

Ancient texts such as the Shiv Swarodaya, Vijnana Bhairava Tantra, and Patanjali Yoga Sutras offer a wealth of knowledge on breath control and other yogic practices. In this book, we'll delve into specific breathing techniques to harness the power of our minds and manifest our desires.

The human body is said to possess 72,000 subtle energy channels, or nadis, originating from the navel and branching out symmetrically. Three of these nadis, Ida, Pingala, and Sushumna, are particularly significant. Ida, often called the Moon Nadi, is associated with feminine energy, while Pingala, or the Sun Nadi, is linked to masculine energy.

Our breathing patterns are closely tied to these nadis. At any given time, one nostril is more active than the other. When the right nostril is dominant, Pingala Nadi is active. When the left nostril is dominant, Ida Nadi is active. A brief period of balanced breathing through both nostrils occurs for few minutes, during which Sushumna Nadi is activated. The human body is made of five elements (tattvas) - Space, Air, Fire, Water, Earth. The Tattvas flow one by one in Ida and Pingala.

Ancient texts like the Shiv Swarodaya provides various practices and lifestyle adjustments based on the active nadi and tattvas. For our purposes of manifestation, we'll focus on a simple breathing technique.

The subconscious mind is most receptive early in the morning, right after waking up. This is why Law of Attraction practitioners emphasize visualization and affirmations at this time to imprint desires onto the subconscious.

A Mindful Approach to Affirmations

Many people make the mistake of continuously repeating affirmations without considering the power of breath. There's no need for constant asking. Instead, focus on a specific morning ritual:

Identify the Active Nostril: Upon waking, determine which nostril is more active.

Align Your Body and Intentional Breathing: Inhale deeply and turn your face towards the active nostril's side. For at least

9 seconds, hold the breath, imagine/visualize your desire, and exhale slowly.

Mindful Rising: As you rise, place the foot corresponding to the active nostril first. Before placing the first foot, begin the inhale-imagine/visualize process for at least 9 seconds. Then keep the other foot, get up and then exhale.

This practice helps program your subconscious mind and balancing of energies within you. Trust that the Universe has heard your request, and let go to embrace your day.

Chapter 2
Unveiling the Connection: Law of Attraction and Lalita Sahasranama

*

This chapter delves into the fascinating connection between the Law of Attraction and the relevant verses of Lalita Sahasranama, exploring how both principles encourage mindful manifestation.

Verse 130 serves as a culminating point, offering a blueprint or formula for harnessing the universal energy to manifest desires.

Verses 1-3 establish the foundational nature of universal energy and its operational principles.

Verses 4-11 explore the human interface with this energy, emphasizing the role of the senses as conduits.

Verse 172 emphasizes the significance of gratitude in our daily lives and importance of cultivating a thankful heart.

Note: These are just one interpretation of the verses. There are many other possible interpretations. It is important to remember that the meaning of a verse is not fixed. It can change depending on the context in which it is chanted or read. The most important thing is to find an interpretation that resonates with you and helps you to connect with the divine.

VERSE 130

**Ichchhā-śaktī-gñyānā-śaktī-krīya-śaktī-sva-rūpiṇī,
Sarv'ādhārā,Su-pratiṣhṭhā,Sad-asad-rūpa-dhārinī. (130)**

Ichchhā-śaktī-gñyānā-śaktī-krīya-śaktī-sva-rūpiṇī

Meaning: "Embodied as the power of Desire, Knowledge and Action"

Sarv'ādhārā

Meaning: "The Support of everything"

Su-pratiṣhṭhā

Meaning: "Firmly established"

Sad-asad-rūpa-dhārinī

Meaning: "The upholder of real and unreal forms"

The Divine as the Manifestor

The Verse beautifully posits the Divine as the embodiment of the powers, suggesting that she is the ultimate manifestor. The verse is interpreted as She who is the form of the power of desire, the power of knowledge, and the power of action; the well-established support of everything; the holder of both the real and the unreal forms. She is the foundation upon which all existence rests, encompassing both the real and unreal forms.

The Alignment Principle in Practice

This verse, rich in philosophical and spiritual connotations, offers profound insights that align remarkably with the core principles of the Law of Attraction:

Ichchhā-śhaktī (Power of Desire): Desire is the driving force behind creation. The Law of Attraction states that what we focus on and desire, we attract into our lives. This verse highlights the divine feminine as the source of all desire, suggesting that our desires are connected to a universal creative force.

Gñyānā-śhaktī (Power of Knowledge): Knowledge empowers us to shape our reality. Understanding the Law of Attraction provides us with the knowledge to consciously create our lives. The divine feminine, as the embodiment of knowledge, guides us towards understanding the underlying principles of manifestation.

Krīya-śhaktī (Power of Action): Action is the bridge between desire and manifestation. The Law of Attraction emphasizes the importance of taking inspired action to bring our desires into reality. The divine feminine, being the power of action, inspires us to take the necessary steps to manifest our dreams.

Sarv'ādhārā Su-pratiṣhṭhā (Well-established support of everything): This phrase suggests that everything in existence is supported by a divine principle. In the context of the Law of Attraction, this principle is the universal law of attraction itself.

Sad-asad-rūpa-dhārinī (Holder of both the real and the unreal forms): This indicates the divine ability to encompass both the manifested and unmanifested realms. This aligns with the concept of the quantum field in physics, where all possibilities exist before they manifest.

Embrace the Essence

In essence, the verse offers a spiritual and philosophical foundation for the Law of Attraction. It suggests that by aligning with the Divine energy, we can tap into the creative power of the universe to manifest our desires.

VERSE 1

Śhrī-mātā,Śhrī-mahā-rājñī,Śhrī-mat-siṁhʿāsanʿeśhvarī, Chid-agni-kuṇḍa-sambhūtā,Deva-kārya-samudyatā. (1)

Śhrī-mātā

Meaning: "The Supreme Mother"

Śhrī-mahā-rājñī

Meaning: "The Supreme Queen"

Śhrī-mat-siṁhʿāsanʿeśhvarī

Meaning: "The Supreme Ruler Seated on the Lion Throne"

Chid-agni-kuṇḍa-sambhūtā

Meaning: "Born from the Fire Altar of Consciousness"

Deva-kārya-samudyatā

Meaning: "Engaged in the Work of the Devas"

The Mother's Embrace: Lalita Sahasranama

Like a child instinctively calling out to their mother in times of joy or hardship, the Lalita Sahasranama begins by invoking the universal mother, Lalita Devi, as **"Śhrī-mātā"** (the Revered Mother - the Universal Energy). She is the source of all creation, both physical and subtle. Each and everything in the universe is created from the same source. The first names in the hymn highlight her creative power (first name) and sustaining power (second name). Envisioned as a mother riding a lion, Lalita Devi embodies both creation and dissolution. The lion, often interpreted as both ferociousness and fearlessness, symbolizes her ability to dissolve negativity and transform devotees. The fourth name describes her as **"Chid-agni-kuṇḍa-sambhūtā"** meaning "born from the fire altar of pure consciousness." This doesn't imply a literal birth, but rather an awakening of Kundalini - The Divine Energy within the devotee's meditative awareness. This awakening eliminates negativity and fosters divine qualities. Lalita Devi dispels ignorance through her pure consciousness, illuminating the darkness of illusion. She is a source of support for both divine beings (devas) and mortals (jivas). Not only does she offer guidance, but she also empowers the devas and jivas to take action when necessary.

The Alignment Principle in Practice

The excerpt draws parallels between the concepts in the Lalita Sahasranama and the Law of Attraction. It highlights the following connections:

Everything is Energy: Both acknowledge a fundamental universal energy that permeates everything.

The Power of Manifestation: The awakening of Kundalini through meditation resonates with the Law of Attraction's focus on directing our thoughts and energy towards desired outcomes.

Divine Support: Both acknowledge the potential for receiving help and guidance from the universe or higher forces and also acknowledge the courage required for transformation.

Embrace the Essence

Understanding these deeper meanings within the first verse of Lalita Sahasranama emphasizes that the Law of Attraction is not merely a superficial concept but aligns with the universal principles of energy, consciousness, and connection to a higher power. It encourages individuals to challenge limiting beliefs and embrace this knowledge for a more peaceful and fulfilling life. Overall, the passage interprets Lalita Sahasranama through the lens of the Law of Attraction, highlighting the connection between the universal energy, our consciousness, and the ability to manifest our desires.

VERSE 2 & 3

**Udyad-bhānu-sahasrābhā,Chatur-bāhu-samanvitā,
Rāga-swarūpa-paśh'āḍhyā,Krodh'ākār'ānkuśh'ojjvalā. (2)**

**Mano-rūp'ekṣhu-kodaṇḍā,Pañcha-tanmātra-sāyakā,
Nij'āruṇa-prabhā-pūra-majjad-brahmāṇḍa-maṇḍalā. (3)**

Udyad-bhānu-sahasrābhā

Meaning: "She who shines with the radiance of a thousand rising suns"

Chatur-bāhu-samanvitā

Meaning: "She who has four arms"

Rāga-swarūpa-paśh'āḍhyā

Meaning: "She who holds the rope of desires"

Krodh'ākār'ānkuśh'ojjvalā

Meaning: "She who shines with the goad of anger"

Mano-rūp'ekṣhu-kodaṇḍā

Meaning: "She who holds the bow of the mind"

Pañcha-tanmātra-sāyakā

Meaning: "She who has the five arrows of the subtle elements"

Nij'āruṇa-prabhā-pūra-majjad-brahmāṇḍa-maṇḍalā

Meaning: "She who fills the universe with her own red radiance"

Meditating on the Divine Mother

This section encourages meditation on the four-armed form of Devi, adorned with various weapons and radiating immense light. The text explores the symbolism of the "Pasa" (noose) and "Ankusha" (goad), representing the interplay of love and hatred in our lives. It emphasizes transcending these polarities through spiritual practice.

Similarly, the contemplation of the "Kodanda" (bow) and five arrows (flowers) serves as a reminder of how our minds are influenced by the five senses, leading to the creation of karma. The practice aims to guide us towards breaking free from creating further negative karma and to embrace forgiveness for others and also for ourselves.

Through meditation, when we connect with divine energy, it provides knowledge, illuminates the right path, and transforms our hatred into love, and anger into wisdom. This energy has the ability to correct our shortcomings.

Overall, these seven names (6-12) further illustrate Lalita Devi's divine attributes and powers. She is the source of light, beauty, power, and control. She is the one who helps us to overcome our limitations and to attain true liberation.

Symbolism and Interpretation

The text describes Devi's radiance, red complexion and her four arms holding the goad, noose, sugarcane bow, and five arrows. These elements are interpreted as follows:

The Radiance of a Thousand Suns: A thousand rising suns represent the infinite potential of cosmic energy.

The Goad: Represents the divine nudge towards the right path for her devotees and the the control and ability to fulfill desires.

The Noose: Represents the power to dispel hatred and bestow knowledge.

The Sugarcane Bow: Symbolizes the crushing of the ego and revealing the sweet reality of Brahman (absolute reality).

The Five Arrows (Flowers): Apart from five senses, five arrows also represent - excitement, madness, confusion, stimulation, and destruction - which can create illusion. Devi uses these "arrows" as her toys to sport **"THE LEELA."**

Red Complexion: The description of Devi's red complexion signifies her universal care and compassion as the mother of all. Red is a color of intense energy, vitality, and power. Devi's red complexion signifies her dynamic and active nature. She is not a passive entity but a force that actively engages with the universe.

The Alignment Principle in Practice

The passage draws parallels between this interpretation and the Law of Attraction

Universal Energy: Our thoughts and emotions, like the energy described in the text, have immense potential.

Functional Nature: The four arms symbolize the various ways this energy works, not literal physical limbs.

Overcoming Negativity: Similar to the noose and goad, the Law of Attraction suggests releasing negative thoughts and embracing positive ones.

Harnessing the Senses: Both concepts acknowledge the role of our senses in influencing our thoughts and desires.

From Thought to Reality: Both emphasize the power of thoughts in shaping our experiences.

Embrace the Essence

In conclusion, these verses delves into the symbolic meaning of Devi's form, connecting it to the principles of the Law of Attraction. It highlights the concept of harnessing our thoughts and emotions to navigate life's journey effectively.

VERSE 4

**Champak'āśhoka-punnāga-saugandhika-lasat-kachā,
Kuruvinda-maṇi-śhreṇī-kanat-koṭīra-maṇḍitā. (4)**

Champak'āśhoka-punnāga-saugandhika-lasat-kachā

Meaning: "She whose hair is adorned with Champaka, Ashoka, Punnaga, and Saugandhika flowers"

Kuruvinda-maṇi-śhreṇī-kanat-koṭīra-maṇḍitā

Meaning: "She who is adorned with a string of Kuruvinda rubies on the crown of her head"

Inner Transformation and High Vibrations

This section focuses on Devi's adorned flowers and a gem, offering deeper meanings

Flowers and Hairs: The four fragrant flowers adorning Devi's hair symbolize the four aspects of our "antahkarana" (inner instrument): mind, intellect, consciousness, and ego. However, they gain their fragrance not from themselves but from Devi's hair, representing the transformation that occurs when we "burn our ego" (overcome negativity) and use our inner faculties in service of higher consciousness. This aligns with the concept of a spiritually elevated yogi's body odor arising not from external substances but from the inner transformation.

Ruby and Forehead: The "Kuruvinda" ruby signifies love, prosperity, and devotion. Meditating on the head of Devi adorned with this gem symbolizes the potential to increase devotion through such contemplation.

The Alignment Principle in Practice

Drawing parallels to the Law of Attraction

High Vibrational State: Similar to the previous interpretations, the text equates a "high vibrational state" with a sweet-smelling state. It emphasizes that through meditation, we can tap into this energy and elevate our vibration. This state of high vibrational energy is achieved by "burning the ego" and using our internal faculties positively, aligning with the concept of positive thoughts attracting positive experiences.

Focusing on Inner Light: The text alludes to meditating on the top of the head (Sahasrara Chakra) to raise consciousness and vibrations, connecting it to the "Kuruvinda" gem. This aligns with the Law of Attraction principle of focusing on our desired state and intentions to manifest them.

Embrace the Essence

Overall, this passage interprets Lalita Sahasranama through the lens of the Law of Attraction, highlighting the importance of inner transformation, overcoming ego, and raising our vibrational state through meditation and positive intent.

VERSE 5

**Aṣhṭamī-chandra-vibhrāja-dalika-sthala-śhobhitā,
Mukha-chandra-kalaṅkābha-mṛiga-nābhi-viśheṣhakā. (5)**

Aṣhṭamī-chandra-vibhrāja-dalika-sthala-śhobhitā

Meaning: "She whose forehead shines beautifully like the moon on the eighth day"

Mukha-chandra-kalaṅkābha-mṛiga-nābhi-viśheṣhakā

Meaning: "She whose face is like the moon, marked with the musky scent of a deer"

Symbolism of the Forehead and Musk on the Forehead

This section delves into the symbolism of Lalita Devi's forehead

Moon on the Eighth Day: Comparing her forehead to the moon on the eighth day of a lunar cycle signifies maintaining mental equanimity regardless of life's circumstances. The moon, associated with the mind in Indian tradition, appears similar on both the light and dark sides of the moon, symbolizing the need for a balanced and calm mind in both good and bad times.

Musk on the Forehead: The "Mriga-nābhi" (musk from a musk deer) on the forehead alludes to maintaining a beautiful mind filled with positive thoughts, attitude, peace. In Tantric traditions, musk is worn on the forehead for this symbolic purpose as a reminder that mind can have negative influences but one need to have self-control.

The Alignment Principle in Practice

Drawing parallels to the Law of Attraction

Maintaining a High Vibrational State: One of the principles shared in the Law of Attraction is staying calm and relaxed to facilitate manifestation. This aligns with the concept of maintaining mental equanimity regardless of the situation, as emphasized in the interpretation.

Controlling Negative Thoughts: The interpretation emphasizes the importance of letting go of negative thoughts and maintaining positive mental states. This aligns with the Law of Attraction principle of attracting positive experiences by focusing on positive thoughts and intentions.

Embrace the Essence

Overall, this passage interprets Lalita Sahasranama through the lens of the Law of Attraction, highlighting the importance of maintaining a balanced and positive mind for successful manifestation and a fulfilling life.

VERSE 6

Vadana-smara-māṅgalya-gṛiha-toraṇa-chillikā,
Vaktra-lakshmi-parīvāha-chalan-mīn'ābha-lochanā. (6)

Vadana-smara-māṅgalya-gṛiha-toraṇa-chillikā

Meaning: "The one whose face is like the glorious palace of the Cupid (The God of Love) and her eyebrows are the entrance arches of that palace"

Vaktra-lakshmi-parīvāha-chalan-mīn'ābha-lochanā

Meaning: "The one whose eyes are like moving fish, resembling the procession of the goddess of wealth"

Symbolism of the Face, Eyebrows and Eyes and Divine Connection

This section explores the symbolic meaning of Lalita Devi's facial features

Face, Eyebrows and Eyes: This verse describes the beauty of Lalita Devi's face, eyebrows and eyes. The face is compared with the house of Cupid which represent love for all. It depicts the loving and happy face. Her eyebrows are like the auspicious garland of Cupid at the door of the house of happiness. This means that she brings happiness to everyone who seeks her. Her eyes are like moving fish in the pool of the goddess of wealth. This means that her eyes are full of life and beauty. Mere glance of her eyes, bestows happiness.

The Alignment Principle in Practice

Drawing parallels to the Law of Attraction

Love and Happiness: The description of Lalita Devi's eyebrows as being like the auspicious garland of Cupid at the door of the house of happiness can be interpreted as a reminder that we should focus on love and happiness in our lives to get love and happiness.

Life and Beauty: The description of her eyes as being like moving fish can be interpreted as a reminder that we should appreciate the beauty of life and also depicts focused attention and visualisation. This suggests that the grace of the divine can provide us with everything.

Embrace the Essence

Overall, this interpretation uses Lalita Devi's facial features as symbolic representations of the power of love, happiness, focused attention, divine grace, and visualization in achieving spiritual and material fulfillment.

VERSE 7

Nava-champaka-puṣhpābha-nāsā-ḍaṇḍa-virājitā,
Tārā-kānti-tiras-kāri-nāsā-bharaṇa-bhāsurā. (7)

Nava-champaka-puṣhpābha-nāsā-ḍaṇḍa-virājitā

Meaning: "The one whose nose is like a new champaka flower, adorned with a nose stud"

Tārā-kānti-tiras-kāri-nāsā-bharaṇa-bhāsurā

Meaning: "Her nose ornament is brighter than the stars, which is a symbol of her power and radiance"

Symbolism of the Nose and Nose Stud and Divine Connection

This section focuses on Devi's nose and nose stud, offering hidden meanings

Nose: Compared to a Champaka flower bud, known for its pure fragrance. This signifies the importance of seeking out and embracing positive influences for spiritual growth. The nose is how we breathe, drawing in sustenance. Similarly, we should nourish our spirit by engaging in good deeds and avoiding negativity, even if enticing. Tantra suggests flower gardens, like those filled with Champaka flowers, as conducive to spiritual practice due to their positive energy.

Nose Stud: Described as brighter than stars, suggesting its ability to ward off the negativity associated with astrological influences.

The Alignment Principle in Practice

Drawing parallels to the Law of Attraction

Positive Thoughts and Actions: Manifestation requires more than just visualization. Our senses play a role, with positive experiences like pleasant smells (Champaka flowers) encouraging positive choices.

Rejecting Negativity: The text emphasizes rejecting negative thoughts and embracing positive ones, similar to inhaling good and exhaling the bad during manifestation and various breathing techniques.

Deep Meditation: Meditation is suggested as a way to experience positive energy and develop the ability to control negative actions.

Embrace the Essence

The verse can be interpreted as a reminder that we should always strive to be beautiful and pure, both in our physical appearance and in our thoughts and actions by encouraging positive choices. We must create positive environment around us. We should also strive to be radiant and powerful, like Lalita Devi.

This verse possesses significant esoteric meaning, especially in the context of yogic breathing practices. The Vigyan Bhairav Tantra and Shiv Swarodaya are primary texts exploring this knowledge. The previously detailed steps on manifestation correspond to a specific technique for materialization.

VERSE 8

**Kadamba-mañjari-klṛipta-karṇa-pūra-manoharā,
Tāṭanka-yugalī-bhūta-tapan-oḍupa-maṇḍalā. (8)**

Kadamba-mañjari-klṛipta-karṇa-pūra-manoharā

Meaning: "Her ears are adorned with clusters of Kadamba flowers, which are more charming than the moon"

Tāṭanka-yugalī-bhūta-tapan-oḍupa-maṇḍalā

Meaning: "The earrings made of sun and moon discs destroy the darkness of ignorance"

The Blossoming of Divinity: Kadamba Flowers and Celestial Earrings

This section focuses on Devi's Ears, Kadamba Flowers and Earrings, offering hidden meanings

Ears adorned with Kadamba Flowers: Lalita Devi wears Kadamba flowers over her ears, known for their fragrant scent. These symbolize surrendering to positive energy during manifestation. The verse can be interpreted as a reminder that we should always strive to be beautiful and pure, both in our physical appearance and in our thoughts and actions. It also represents that we should create and seek a peaceful environment around us. We should listen to divine chants.

Earrings: These symbolize Lalita Devi's control over the universe, as the sun and moon govern life cycles. This verse hints at the activation of Ida (Moon Nadi), Pingala (Surya Nadi), and Sushumna nadis (subtle energy channels) in Kundalini awakening, a Tantric practice for spiritual growth. With the practices like Thoppu Karanam, we can also cleanse our nadis.

The Alignment Principle in Practice

Drawing parallels to the Law of Attraction

Letting Go and Positivity: Manifestation requires withdrawing from negativity and surrendering to divine energy, similar to experiencing the positive fragrance of Kadamba flowers. The residence of Kadamba groves represent that one should create and seek positive environment and pay attention to divine words, positive opinions rejecting the negative ones.

Mindfulness and Relaxation: Practices like Thoppu Karanam (Super Brain Yoga) help calm the mind during manifestation, similar to the calming effect of relaxation techniques used in the Law of Attraction.

Embrace the Essence

This verse is a beautiful and powerful verse that can help us to connect with Lalita Devi and her divine energy. By chanting this verse, we can increase our beauty and purity, dispel the darkness of ignorance, and gain enlightenment.

VERSE 9

Padma-rāga-śhil'ādarśha-pari-bhāvi-kapola-bhūḥ,
Nava-vidruma-bimba-śhrī-nyak-kāri-radanach-chhadā. (9)

Padma-rāga-śhil'ādarśha-pari-bhāvi-kapola-bhūḥ

Meaning: "Her cheeks are like a mirror reflecting the red Padmaraga gemstone"

Nava-vidruma-bimba-śhrī-nyak-kāri-radanach-chhadā

Meaning: "Her lips, which are red like the Bimba fruit, are like a beautiful umbrella protecting her teeth"

The Blossoming of Divinity: Cheeks and Lips

This section focuses on Devi's Cheeks and Lips offering hidden meanings

Cheeks: It describes the beauty of Lalita Devi's cheeks. Her cheeks are compared to a red Padmaraga gemstone, symbolizing their radiance and beauty.Described as rosy, symbolizing liveliness and love. It suggests meditating on their vibrant color to increase one's own vitality.

Lips: Said to outshine coral and Bimba fruit (known for red color). Meditating on their reddish hue is believed to enhance the power and beauty of one's speech.

The Alignment Principle in Practice

Drawing parallels to the Law of Attraction

Happiness and Success: According to the Law of Attraction, maintaining a positive, happy mindset (represented by red cheeks) is crucial for manifestation. Happiness doesn't come from material fulfillment; self-love, love for others, liveliness is the foundation for achieving it.

Speech and Awareness: Our words and communication style play a significant role in manifesting desires. The verse emphasizes the importance of using positive, mindful language, similar to how meditation on Lalita Devi's lips enhances speech.

Embrace the Essence

This verse beautifully describes Lalita Devi's features while offering subtle connections to the Law of Attraction through themes of positive energy, attractive qualities, and mindful communication.

VERSE 10

**Śhuddha-vidyʻānkur-ākāra-dvija-pankti-dvayʻojjvalā,
Karpūra-vītikā-moda-samākarṣhi-digantarā. (10)**

Śhuddha-vidyʻānkur-ākāra-dvija-pankti-dvayʻojjvalā

Meaning: "Her teeth are like two rows of pure white sprouts, shining brightly"

Karpūra-vītikā-moda-samākarṣhi-digantarā

Meaning: "Her breath is fragrant like camphor, attracting all directions"

The Blossoming of Divinity: Teeth & Breath

This section focuses on Devi's Teeth and her Breath, offering hidden meanings

Teeth: This suggests that the devotee strives to purify their thoughts and speech through Shuddha-Vidya. By meditating on the teeth as the mantra sounds, past negative impressions ("samskaras") are believed to be dissolved, leading to enlightenment and transcendence.

Breath: The camphor completely burns leaving behind a pleasant fragrance, symbolizing the complete dissolution of the three gunas (rajas, tamas, and sattva), leading to the experience of divine light and fragrance. The fragrance may also represent a means to attract devotees. Knowledgeable ones are drawn through devotion, while ignorant ones may be drawn by the initial allure.

The Alignment Principle in Practice

Drawing parallels to the Law of Attraction

Power of Words: Mantras, affirmations, and positive thoughts are tools used in the Law of Attraction to shift our vibration and attract desired outcomes. This connects to the Shuddha -Vidya practice by using sounds to elevate consciousness.

Embrace New Beginnings: This divine energy resides within us, guiding and transforming our lives when negativity reaches a tipping point. It attracts ignorant men. Knowledgeable already know how to invoke this energy. When negative energy reaches a certain level, the Law of Attraction suggests that our inner guidance takes over to initiate positive change. Many examples exist of individuals overcoming challenges and experiencing significant positive change. This aligns with the concept of the divine energy within us guiding us after experiencing a period of darkness (the negative energy). Also, The fragrance of camphor is associated with freshness and renewal. This verse could be seen as a reminder to embrace new beginnings and let go of negativity, which can help us manifest our desires more easily.

Embrace the Essence

The Verse highlights the purity and freshness associated with Lalita Devi's teeth and breath, while offering connections to the Law of Attraction through themes of positive qualities, new beginnings, and letting go of negativity.

- 65 -

VERSE 11

**Nija-sallāpa-mādhurya-vinir-bhartsita-kachchhapī,
Manda-smita-prabhāpūra-majjat-kāmeśha-mānasā. (11)**

Nija-sallāpa-mādhurya-vinir-bhartsita-kachchhapī

Meaning: "The sweetness of whose discourse puts to shame the Veena of Saraswati"

Manda-smita-prabhāpūra-majjat-kāmeśha-mānasā

Meaning: "The one into whose gentle and entrancing smile the mind of Shiva is drowned"

The Power of Lalita Devi's speech and Entrancing Smile

This section focuses on Devi's speech and her smile, offering hidden meanings

Speech: This refers to the quality of speech. Positive, affirming and loving words resonate at a high vibrational frequency, attracting positive experiences. The description - Putting to shame the Veena of Saraswati is a metaphor for the extraordinary power of spoken words. Just as the music of a Veena is enchanting, so too are words when used consciously and positively.

Smile: A smile is a powerful emotional expression. A gentle and loving smile emits a high vibrational frequency, attracting positive energy. Shiva is often depicted as without passions.

This verse describes that the gentle smile has the power to seduce anyone.

The Alignment Principle in Practice

Drawing parallels to the Law of Attraction

Vibration and Frequency: The sweetness of speech is akin to a high vibrational frequency. The Law of Attraction posits that what we focus on, we attract. Thus, sweet and positive words resonate at a higher frequency, attracting positive experiences.

Manifestation through Words: The verse suggests that words have the power to create reality. This aligns with the Law of Attraction's principle that our thoughts and words become things.

Emotional Vibration: The gentle and entrancing smile is a symbol of positive emotion. The Law of Attraction emphasizes the importance of emotions in manifestation. Positive emotions raise our vibrational frequency, attracting positive experiences and positive outcomes.

Embrace the Essence

The Verse emphasizes the importance of our thoughts, words, and emotions in creating our reality. They align perfectly with the core principles of the Law of Attraction: that like attracts like, and that our vibrational frequency determines our experiences. By consciously choosing our thoughts, words, and emotions, we can harness the power of attraction to manifest a life of abundance, happiness, and fulfillment.

VERSE 172

**Stotra-priyā,Stuti-matī,Śhruti-saṁ-stuta-vaibhavā,
Manasvinī,Māna-vatī,Maheśhī-Maṅgal'ākṛitiḥ. (172)**

Stotra-priyā

Meaning: "One who loves hymns or praises"

Stuti-matī

Meaning: "Praiseworthy"

Śhruti-saṁ-stuta-vaibhavā

Meaning: "Whose Greatness is extolled in the scriptures"

Manasvinī

Meaning: "Controlling the mind"

Māna-vatī

Meaning: "Highly honoured"

Maheśhī-Maṅgal'ākṛitiḥ.

Meaning: "The Great Goddess"

The Esoteric View of Gratitude

This section focuses on the importance of Gratitude in our journey of life.

Overall Meaning: When we combine all names in the verse, we get a vivid image of the goddess who loves hymns and praises, worthy of being praised and her glory is narrated in the scriptures. She controls the mind, the essence of mind and possess supereme dignity. She is the consort of Shiva, the auspicious one. Manas in the verse, is the pre-rational mind which forms our conditionings, not the intellect which is Buddhi.

Deeper Significance: Regardless of the term we use - thankfulness, gratitude, praise, or appreciation -its esoteric essence extends beyond mere acknowledgment of blessings. It's a transformative spiritual practice that bridges us to a higher power, be it divine or universal helping us see the blessings around us and find our place in the universe.

The Alignment Principle in Practice

Drawing parallels to the Law of Attraction

Alignment with Divine Will: Gratitude aligns us with the divine plan or cosmic order. When we express gratitude, we acknowledge that everything that happens, both positive and negative, is part of a larger, interconnected tapestry.

Surrender: Gratitude can be a form of surrender, letting go of resistance and trusting in the divine's wisdom.

Cultivating Abundance: The law of attraction suggests that what we focus on expands. By focusing on gratitude, we attract more abundance into our lives, not just in material terms but also in terms of love, joy and peace. Gratitude shifts our perspective from lack to abundance, allowing us to see the blessings in our lives, no matter how small.

Deepening connection with the Divine: Gratitude can be a channel for divine grace. When we express gratitude, we open ourselves to receive the blessings of the universe. Gratitude can be a form of prayer or meditation. It connects us with a higher power and can lead to a sense of peace and tranquility.

Transmuting Negative Emotions: Gratitude can counteract negative emotions like anger, fear, and resentment. It shifts our focus away from what is wrong and towards what is right. Gratitude can be a powerful tool for healing, both physically and emotionally. It can help us to release negative energy and cultivate positive vibrations. Gratitude reminds us of our interconnectedness with all beings and the universe. It fosters a sense of unity and compassion.

Embrace the Essence

The Verse emphasizes the importance of Gratitude in creating our reality. Gratitude is a spiritual practice that can lead to greater happiness, peace, and fulfillment. By cultivating gratitude, we can deepen our connection with the divine, attract more abundance into our lives, and live in harmony with the universe.

Chapter 3
Healing Within: Chakra Meditation

———— ✳ ————

This chapter explores the concepts of spiritual healing and chakra meditation, focusing specifically on verses 38-40 of Lalita Sahasranama and their role in fostering inner well-being and self-realisation.

INTRODUCTION TO CHAKRAS

These verses introduces Kundalini, a powerful, formless energy believed to reside at the base of the spine. It awakens through spiritual practices like meditation and healing techniques. It emphasizes the potential of spiritual practices like meditation and healing to foster self-awareness and well-being.

The focus then shifts to the seven main chakras, considered the most prominent energy centers within the human body. While various spiritual traditions acknowledge a broader network of chakras, the seven mentioned in this book are the most widely recognized and interconnected, influencing our physical, emotional, and spiritual well-being.

It's important to acknowledge that the concept of chakras, including the number, location, and function of minor and micro chakras, is complex and varies across different spiritual traditions. There is ongoing debate and no single, universally accepted definition or diagram encompassing all aspects of the chakra system.

These verses focuses on understanding the seven main chakras and further describes the journey of Kundalini shakti, a powerful energy within us, as it awakens and ascends through the seven chakras, leading to spiritual transformation.

Awakening: Kundalini starts at the base chakra (Muladhara), symbolizing stability, and pierces the first knot (Brahma granthi) representing release from ignorance. The two chakras Muladhara and Swadishthana, together are said to represent the Brahma Granthi.

Moving Upward: It rises to the Manipura chakra (personal power) and dissolves duality/ego (Vishnu granthi). The two chakras Manipura and Anahata, together are said to represent the Vishnu Granthi.

Clarity and Beyond: Upon reaching the Ajna chakra, also known as the "Third eye," Kundalini pierces the third knot, the Rudra granthi. This breakthrough leads to clarity of vision, destroying illusion and allowing us to perceive reality directly. The Vishuddhi and Ajna chakras are considered together as the Rudra Granthi.

Bliss and Union: Finally, it reaches the crown chakra (Sahasrara), symbolizing enlightenment, and showers "nectar" representing the ultimate goal of spiritual experience - healing, complete union and self-realization.

VERSE 38

**Mūlādhār'aika-nilayā,Brahma-granthi-vibhedinī
Maṇipur'āntar-uditā,Viṣhṇu-granthi-vibhedinī. (38)**

Mūlādhār'aika-nilayā

Meaning: "The one dwelling in the root chakra"

Interpretation: The Kundalini shakti resides in the Muladhara chakra, which is located at the base of the spine. This chakra is associated with the element of earth and represents stability, security, and grounding.

Brahma-granthi-vibhedinī

Meaning: "That which breaks the knot of Brahma"

Interpretation: The knot of Brahma signifies the illusion of separateness from the divine. It is the belief that the individual soul is separate from the supreme reality. The "destruction of the knot of Brahma" refers to the realization of the oneness of the individual soul with the supreme reality. The two chakras Muladhara and Swadishthana, together are said to represent the Brahma Granthi.

Maṇipur'āntar-uditā

Meaning: "The one who rises in the Manipura Chakra"

Interpretation: The Kundalini shakti then rises to the Manipura chakra, which is located in the navel region. This chakra is associated with the element of fire and represents personal power, willpower, and transformation.

Viṣṇu-granthi-vibhedinī

Meaning: "That which breaks the knot of Vishnu"

Interpretation: She who rises within the navel chakra is the one who pierces the knot of Vishnu. The Kundalini shakti then pierces the Vishnu granthi, which is a knot of duality. The knot of Vishnu also represents the attachment to the ego. This knot is located at the Manipura chakra. The two chakras Manipura and Anahata, together are said to represent the Vishnu Granthi.

Overall Interpretation

The verse is describing the Kundalini energy, which is a powerful force of transformation that resides at the base of the spine. When it is awakened, it rises up the spine, piercing through the seven chakras, or energy centers, in the body. As it rises, it dissolves the knots that bind us to our lower nature, allowing us to experience higher states of consciousness.

The two lines of the verse 38 specifically refer to the two chakras, the Muladhara and Manipura. The Muladhara chakra is associated with the physical body and the root instinct of survival. The Manipura chakra is associated with the ego and the sense of personal power.

When the Kundalini pierces through the Muladhara chakra, it releases us from our attachment to the physical world and allows us to experience a deeper sense of connection to our true nature. When it pierces through the Manipura chakra, it dissolves our ego and helps us to develop a more balanced and compassionate sense of self.

The Kundalini energy is a powerful force that can bring about profound transformation in our lives. If we are willing to work with it, it can help us to awaken to our full potential and experience the highest states of consciousness.

VERSE 39

**Agñyā-chakr'āntarāla-sthā,Rudra-granthi-vibhedinī
Sahasrār'āmbuj'ārūḍhā,Sudhā-sār'ābhi-varṣhiṇī. (39)**

Agñyā-chakr'āntarāla-sthā

Meaning: "That who is situated in the space between the Ajna chakras"

Interpretation: The Kundalini shakti then moves to the Ajna chakra, which is located between the eyebrows. This chakra is associated with the element of light and represents intuition, perception, and clarity of mind.

Rudra-granthi-vibhedinī

Meaning: "That which breaks the knot of Rudra"

Interpretation: The Kundalini shakti then pierces the Rudra granthi, which is a knot of illusion. This knot is located at the Ajna chakra. The two chakras Vishuddhi and Ajna, together are said to represent the Rudra Granthi.

Sahasrār'āmbuj'ārūḍhā

Meaning: "That who ascends the lotus of the Sahasrara chakra"

Interpretation: The Kundalini shakti then ascends to the Sahasrara chakra, which is located at the crown of the head. This chakra is associated with the element of spirit and represents enlightenment, union with God, and pure consciousness.

Sudhā-sārʻābhi-varṣhiṇī

Meaning: "The one who showers the essence of nectar"

Interpretation: The Kundalini shakti showers the essence of nectar, which is the bliss of healing, enlightenment, union with God, and pure consciousness which is the ultimate goal of spiritual development.

Overall Interpretation

The two lines of the verse specifically refer to the sixth and seventh chakras, the Ajna and Sahasrara. The Ajna chakra is associated with the mind and the ability to see beyond illusion. The Sahasrara chakra is associated with pure consciousness and spiritual enlightenment.

When the Kundalini pierces through the Ajna chakra, it opens our third eye and allows us to see the world with greater clarity and insight, shattering illusion. When it pierces through the Sahasrara chakra, we experience the ultimate state of union with divine consciousness. The Kundalini shakti then showers the essence of nectar, which is the bliss of healing, enlightenment, union with God, and pure consciousness which is the ultimate goal of spiritual development.

VERSE 40

Taḍillata-sama-ruchiḥ,Ṣhat-chakrʻopari-samsthitā
Mahā-śhaktiḥ,Kuṇḍalinī,Bisa-tantu-tanīyasī. (40)

Taḍillata-sama-ruchiḥ

Meaning: "That who appears like lightning"

Interpretation: The Kundalini shakti has a radiance like lightning. This indicates her power and transformative potential.

Ṣhat-chakrʻopari-samsthitā

Meaning: "That who is situated above the six chakras"

Interpretation: The Kundalini shakti is situated above the six chakras. This indicates that she has transcended the limitations of the material world and is now in the realm of spirit.

Mahā-śhaktiḥ-Kuṇḍalinī

Meaning: "That who is the great power, Kundalini"

Interpretation: The Kundalini shakti is the great power. The Kundalini shakti, the very essence of creation and the driving force behind spiritual growth, transcends the six chakras. Now residing in the Sahasrara, the crown chakra, the chakra of Shiva - it symbolizes the state of divine union - ultimate bliss.

Bisa-tantu-tanīyasī

Meaning: "That one who is as fine as a thread of fibre stalk"

Interpretation: The Kundalini shakti is as subtle as a lightning thread. This indicates her delicate and elusive nature.

Overall Interpretation

The verse is describing the Kundalini energy, which is a powerful force of transformation that resides at the base of the spine. It is said to be coiled like a serpent and is often depicted as a lightning bolt. The verse also mentions that the Kundalini is situated above the six chakras, which are energy centers in the body.

The Kundalini energy is a powerful force that can bring about profound transformation in our lives. If we are willing to work with it, it can help us to awaken to our full potential and experience the highest states of consciousness. However, she is also elusive, requiring a great deal of dedication and spiritual practice.

The description of Lalita Devi as Kundalini can be interpreted as a reminder that we all have the potential to awaken our own inner power. The description of her leading us to enlightenment can be interpreted as a reminder that we can manifest our desires by connecting with our divine source.

Additional Interpretation to verses 38, 39 and 40

The verses 38-40 can also be interpreted as a description of the process of spiritual enlightenment. The three knots mentioned in the verses 38 and 39 represent the three main obstacles that we must overcome on the spiritual path:

The knot of Brahma represents the attachment to the physical world. The knot of Vishnu represents the attachment to the ego. The knot of Rudra represents the attachment to the mind.

When we pierce through these knots, we are free from the limitations of the lower self and can experience the true nature of reality.

These verses also describes the two main fruits of spiritual enlightenment:

The nectar that showers down from the crown chakra represents the bliss of divine union.

The clear vision that comes from opening the third eye represents the wisdom of true understanding.

These verses constitute a beautiful and poetic exposition of the spiritual enlightenment journey, underscoring the arduous nature of the path while emphasizing the significant rewards of ultimate happiness and fulfillment attainable through diligent application.

The verse 40 can also be interpreted as a description of the divine energy. The lightning bolt is a symbol of power and transformation, and the serpent is a symbol of wisdom and healing. The verse suggests that the divine energy is a powerful force that can bring about transformation and healing in our lives.

The verse 40 also mentions that the Kundalini is situated above the six chakras. The chakras are energy centers in the body that are associated with different aspects of our physical, emotional, and spiritual well-being. The verse suggests that the divine energy is a source of energy and vitality that can help us to achieve balance and harmony in all aspects of our lives.

The term "Bisatantu" refers to the network of subtle nerves that permeate the human body. According to the text, these nadis number 72,000 and are invisible to the naked eye. Among the body's 72,000 subtle energy channels, or nadis, Ida, Pingala, and Sushumna are the primary ones. The intersections of these three nadis correspond to the seven major chakras described in these verses.

When the union of Shiva and Shakti occurs within the practitioner, the resulting torrent of bliss is said to flow through this network of nadis.

This flow is described as drenching the entire body, bringing an unspeakable state of bliss and promotes healing.

Chapter 4
Activating the Chakras: Unveiling the Chakra Meditation Process

This chapter unveils the secrets of chakra meditation, providing a step-by-step guide to activate your energy centers for holistic healing.

Spiritual Healing: A Journey Beyond Material Manifestation

While some principles of self-care and positive thinking might overlap with the Law of Attraction when it comes to manifesting material things, it's important to understand that spiritual healing involves a deeper and more holistic approach.

Key Practices for Spiritual Healing

Self-love and acceptance: Cultivating a foundation of self-compassion is crucial for healing.

Living in the present moment: Mindfulness helps us release the past and embrace the present, fostering inner peace.

Managing negative emotions: Recognizing and acknowledging negative emotions without dwelling on them is essential for emotional well-being.

Positive thinking and shifting negative beliefs: Cultivating an optimistic outlook while challenging limiting beliefs empowers personal growth.

Faith and trust in a higher power: Whether spiritual or simply a belief in the power within oneself, faith can offer comfort and support.

Healthy Lifestyle: Cultivating a healthy lifestyle is crucial for healing.

Engaging in practices like chakra meditation: These practices can create a sense of inner balance and alignment, contributing to spiritual well-being.

Openness to receiving spiritual energy: This can be seen as a process of becoming receptive to a deeper sense of connection and inner peace.

Gratitude: Expressing gratitude for the healing process, be it through prayers, affirmations, or simply acknowledging progress, can strengthen your resolve and enhance the experience.

STEP-BY-STEP GUIDE TO CHAKRA MEDITATION

Setting the Stage for Transformation

Get comfortable:

Locate a quiet, undisturbed space, whether it's a cozy room in your home, a serene park bench, or anywhere that allows you to fully unwind.

Settle into comfort:

Choose a position that promotes relaxation while maintaining good posture. You can sit cross-legged on the floor or a cushion, kneel, or lie down comfortably on your back.

Set your intention:

Briefly define the purpose of your meditation. This could be focusing on a specific chakra, addressing a particular life challenge, or simply achieving overall balance and well-being in all your energy centers.

Embarking on the Journey

Close your eyes and breathe deeply:

Gently close your eyes and begin with a few minutes of deep breathing. Pay close attention to your breath, feeling the rise and fall of your chest or abdomen with each inhale and exhale. This helps quiet your mind and prepare you for the meditative journey.

Divine Protection Shield:

Imagine/Visualize White/Golden/Red Divine light coming towards you and getting yourself sorrounded by a beautiful warm divine light. This light is not just around your body, but extends a few feet outwards, creating a protecting bubble. Also affirm, that this divine light is protecting you from any harm, danger, accidents, negative energies, and psychic attacks. It protects you at all dimensions of your existence for a duration of a minimum of twenty-four hours.

Connecting with Each Chakra:

Now, visualize/imagine and focus on each chakra, moving upwards from the base of your spine:

Root Chakra (Red): Imagine roots growing from your body, anchoring you firmly to the earth. Visualize/Imagine the color red as you breathe in deeply. Hold the breath. Picture this chakra, located at the base of your spine, as a red lotus flower or spinning disc. Visualise/Imagine vibrant, healing light entering the root chakra. You can silently or aloud say an affirmation like "I am safe and grounded." and then exhale. You can repeat this practice 5-11 times or more.

Sacral Chakra (Orange): Move your attention below your navel, the seat of the Sacral Chakra associated with creativity and emotions. Breathe in deeply, hold the breath - Visualize/Imagine the color orange and say an affirmation like "I am creative and flow with life." and then exhale. You can repeat this practice 5-11 times or more.

Solar Plexus Chakra (Yellow): Continue upwards to the upper abdomen, where the Solar Plexus Chakra resides, governing personal power and confidence. Breathe in deeply, hold the breath - Visualize/Imagine the color yellow and say an affirmation like "I am strong and confident." and then exhale. You can repeat this practice 5-11 times or more.

Heart Chakra (Green): Locate the Heart Chakra in the center of your chest, associated with love and compassion. Breathe in deeply, hold the breath - Visualize/Imagine the color green and say an affirmation like "I am loved and I love." and then exhale. You can repeat this practice 5-11 times or more.

Throat Chakra (Blue): Ascend to the throat, where the Throat Chakra resides, governing communication and self-expression. Breathe deeply, hold the breath - Visualize/Imagine the color blue and repeat say an affirmation like "I speak my truth with clarity." and then exhale. You can repeat this practice 5-11 times or more.

Third Eye Chakra (Indigo): Move between your eyebrows to the Third Eye Chakra, associated with intuition and wisdom. Breathe in deeply, hold the breath -Visualize/Imagine the color indigo and say an affirmation like "I see clearly and trust my intuition." and then exhale. You can repeat this practice 5-11 times or more.

Crown Chakra (Violet): Finally, reach the top of your head, where the Crown Chakra resides, associated with spiritual connection and enlightenment. Breathe in deeply, hold the breath - Visualize/Imagine the color violet and say an affirmation like "I am connected to the universe." and then exhale. You can repeat this practice 5-11 times or more.

Shower of Nectar: Imagine/Visualise a shower of divine nectar, bathing you completely. Feel it flowing through your nerves and every cell, permeating your entire being. This blissful downpour brings healing, enlightenment, a sense of oneness with the divine, and pure consciousness.

Integrating the Journey

Balancing the Chakras: Once you've completed the visualization/Imagination for each chakra, breathe in deeply, imagine them spinning together clockwise, symbolizing balanced energy flow throughout your system and then exhale.

Returning gently: Take a few quiet moments to integrate the experience. Slowly open your eyes and gently wiggle your fingers and toes when you feel ready.

Remember

It's normal for your mind to wander during meditation. Gently guide your attention back to the present moment and your breath.

Be patient and consistent with your practice. Regular meditation can lead to deeper benefits over time.

Explore various resources, such as guided meditations and information about each chakra, their mantras if you want to enhance your understanding and experience. Using Mantras,

Visualisation/Imagination of colours are optional. These are purely for boosting focus and concentration. Intention is the key.

The Lalita Sahasranama further gives description of the chakras in verses 98-110, and the guided meditation that is provided in this book incorporates chakra points and colours based on generally accepted chakra meditation practices. It is important to note that the Lalita Sahasranama itself does not mention the points and colours of the chakras exactly as mentioned in this book.

While incorporating divine energy visualization or imagination can be part of your practice, it's important to remember that chakra meditation is not a substitute for medical treatment. Always prioritize following your doctor's prescribed medications and seek professional medical advice when needed. Doctors are individuals sent by Divine Energy to assist us.

Additional Tips

Deepening Your Chakra Meditation Practice

Here are some additional insights to enhance your experience with chakra meditation:

Embrace the Wandering Mind: It's natural for your thoughts to drift during meditation. Don't get discouraged! Acknowledge the distraction gently and then guide your attention back to your breath or the present moment. This practice strengthens your focus and mindfulness over time.

Cultivate Patience and Consistency: Like any skill, mastering chakra meditation takes time and dedication. Be patient with yourself, and strive for regular practice. Even short, consistent sessions can lead to significant benefits in the long run.

Explore the Abundance of Resources: Delve deeper into the world of chakra meditation! Numerous online resources and libraries offer guided meditations, detailed information about each chakra and other knowledge to enrich your practice and understanding.

BENEFITS OF CHAKRA MEDITATION

Physical Health

Reduced Stress: By promoting relaxation and mindfulness, chakra meditation can help lower stress hormones, potentially leading to improved sleep, digestion, and overall mental and physical health.

Enhanced Energy Levels: Balancing your chakras may improve energy flow within your body, leading to increased vitality and a sense of well-being.

Pain Management: Studies suggest that meditation practices, including chakra meditation, can help manage chronic pain by reducing its emotional impact and improving coping mechanisms.

Mental and Emotional Well being

Increased Focus and Concentration: Focusing on visualization/imagination and affirmations or mantras during meditation can sharpen your focus and improve your ability to concentrate, both in the practice itself and in daily life.

Reduced Anxiety and Depression: By promoting relaxation and fostering positive emotions, chakra meditation can contribute to managing symptoms of anxiety and depression.

Greater Self-Awareness: Paying attention to your thoughts and feelings during meditation can enhance your self-awareness, allowing you to better understand your inner world and emotional patterns.

Improved Emotional Regulation: Through mindfulness and self-awareness gained in meditation, you can develop healthier ways to manage your emotions and respond to life's challenges with greater calmness and resilience.

Deeper Connection to Self: Focusing on different chakras, which represent various aspects of your being, can foster a deeper connection to your authentic self and a sense of inner peace.

Spiritual Awakening: Some practitioners believe that chakra meditation can facilitate spiritual growth by helping to awaken dormant energies and connect with higher levels of consciousness.

It's important to remember that these are potential benefits, and individual experiences may vary. While some studies support the claims listed above, the research on chakra meditation is still ongoing. Consistent practice and a dedicated approach are key to experiencing the full potential benefits of chakra meditation.

Chapter 5
Sri Yantra Meditation: A Guide to Sri Yantra Tratak

This chapter introduces the practice of Sri Yantra meditation, also known as tratak, and explains its benefits for enhancing focus and spiritual growth.

Sri Yantra: A Gateway to the Cosmos Within

The Sri Yantra, a sacred geometric diagram, is believed to encapsulate the very essence of the universe. It's said to be a reflection of the microcosm within us, mirroring the macrocosm of the cosmos outside. This powerful symbol can serve as a potent tool for meditation, guiding you towards inner peace and clarity.

Embarking on the Practice

Unveiling Inner Peace through Sri Yantra Meditation

Seek Serenity: Find a tranquil space free from distractions, allowing you to fully immerse yourself in the experience.

Postural Comfort: Settle into a comfortable sitting position with your spine erect for optimal focus and energy flow.

Gazing at the Yantra: Observe the Sri Yantra, taking in its intricate details. For a more focused experience, consider using a black and white, red, or red and yellow print (preferably 12*12 inches) placed at eye level on a wall three feet away. Gently gaze at the central dot (Bindu) without blinking excessively.

Inner Tranquility: Close your eyes and take deep calming breaths. Feel the rise and fall of your chest as your mind begins to quiet. You can invoke Divine Protection Shield if you wish to.

Visualization: Mentally recreate the image of the Sri Yantra in your mind's eye, fostering a deeper connection with its symbolic essence.

Mindfulness and Manifestation: Embrace a state of present-moment awareness, letting go of any intrusive thoughts or emotions. You can tap into subconscious desires and reprogram your mind for success with affirmations and visualization/imagination. It facilitates the visualization of goals and fuels the motivation to achieve them. Breathe in while stating your desires/affirmation for at least 9 seconds and then breathe out.

Gentle Return: After a few minutes, ease back into your surroundings by slowly opening your eyes and taking a few deep breaths. Consider washing your eyes if needed.

Frequency and Refinement

Practice Sri Yantra meditation as often as feels comfortable, gradually increasing the duration as you become more accustomed to the technique. Remember, this is a personalized journey; adapt the practice to suit your needs and preferences.

While generally considered safe, consulting a healthcare professional before starting any new practice is crucial, especially if you have pre-existing health conditions.

May your exploration of Sri Yantra meditation guide you towards greater self- awareness, inner peace, and the fulfillment of your deepest aspirations.

Benefits of Sri Yantra Meditation

Enhanced Focus and Reduced Stress: By observing the intricate details of the Yantra, your mind becomes more focused, and stress levels naturally decline as you enter a state of calm awareness.

Clarity of Thought and Mind: Focusing on the Yantra promotes mental clarity, enabling you to approach life's challenges with a sharper perspective and renewed purpose.

Goal Manifestation: While not a guaranteed method, Sri Yantra meditation can help you tap into subconscious desires and reprogram your mind for success. It facilitates the visualization of goals and fuels the motivation to achieve them.

Sri Yantra meditation like Chakra Meditation offers a range of other potential benefits, impacting various aspects of your life, from physical well-being to spiritual growth.

While incorporating divine energy visualization or imagination can be part of your practice, it's important to remember that yantra meditation is not a substitute for medical treatment. Always prioritize following your doctor's prescribed medications and seek professional medical advice when needed.

SRI YANTRA

Chapter 6
Lalita Sahasranama: A Divine Elixir

This final chapter presents the complete Lalita Sahasranama for chanting, aiming to unlock its profound wisdom and power.

In Hinduism, the Lalita Sahasranama is a revered hymn enshrined within the Brahmanda Purana. It unfolds the multifaceted essence of the goddess Lalita Devi, also known as Tripura Sundari, through 1000 poetic names/183 poetic verses. Each name, like a brushstroke, paints a unique aspect, quality, or characteristic of the divine.

ŚHRĪ LALITĀ SAHASRA-NĀMA STOTRAM
The Thousand Names of Śhrī Lalitā as a poem

Om Śhrī Gaṇeśhāya namaḥ

'Salutations to the Lord of Ganas and Remover of Obstacles'

Dedication:

Asyā-Śhrī-Lalitā-sahasra-nāma-stotra-mālā-mahā-mantrasya.

Of this garland of mighty mantras of the Thousand Names of Śhrī Lalitā.

Vaśhiny-ādi-vāg-devatā-ṛiṣhayaḥ.

The Composing Seers are Vāśhini and the other Vāg-devatās.

Anuṣhṭup-chhandaḥ.

The metre is Anuṣtubh.

Śhrī-Lalitā-parameśhvarī-devatā.

The Presiding Deity is the Supreme Goddess Śhrī Lalitā.

Aiṁ bījam,Sauḥ śhaktiḥ,Klīṁ kilakam.

Aim is the seed, Sauḥ is the power, Klīm is the door-latch.

Śhrī-Lalitā-mahā-tripura-sundarī-cintitaphalāvāptyarthe-prasād-siddhy-artha-jape viniyogaḥ.

This recitation is undertaken to obtain the desired result of a thought and to please Śhrī Lalitā Mahā-Tripura-Sundarī.

(Impotant Note: Breathe in, hold the breath and then ask for wish and then breathe out)

MEDITATION

Sindūr'āruṇa-vigrahām-tri-nayanām
Māṇikya-mauli-sphurat-tārā-nāyaka-śhekharām
Smita-mukhim-āpīna-vakṣhoruhām.
Pāṇim-yāmali-pūrṇa-ratna-chaṣhakam
Rakt'otpalam-bibhratīm-saumyām-ratna-ghaṭa-stha
Rakta-charaṇām-dhyāyet-par'āmbikām..

I meditate upon the Supreme Mother, red like Sindūr powder, three-eyed, with the crescent Moon as her crest jewel, who isadorned a crown of gems, with an enchanting smiling indicating compassion and have well-formed bosoms. In Her hands she bears a red Lotus, and a precious cup of Nectar. She is cheerful and her red feet rest on a water-pot encrusted with precious stones.

aruṇāṃ-karuṇā-taraṅgitākṣīṃ
dhṛta pāśāṅkuśa puṣpa bāṇacāpām.
aṇimādibhi rāvṛtāṃ mayūkhai-
rahamityeva vibhāvaye bhavānīm..

I meditate upon the Great Empress. She is red in color, and her eyes are full of compassion, and holds the noose, the goad, the bow and the flowery arrows in her hands. She is sorrounded on all sides by powers such as Anima for rays and she is the self within me.

dhyāyet-padmāsanasthāṃ-vikasitavadanā-
padmapatrāyatākṣīṃ
hemābhāṃ-pītavastrāṃ-karakalitalasaddhemapadmāṃ-
varāṅgīm.
sarvālaṅkāra-yuktāṃ-satata-mabhayadāṃ-
bhaktanamrāṃ bhavānīṃ
śrīvidyāṃ-śānta-mūrtiṃ-sakala-suranutāṃ-sarva-
sampatpradātrīm..

I meditate upon the Divine Goddess who is seated on the lotus with petal eyes. She is golden hued, and has a lotus flowers in her hand. She dispels fear of the devotees who bow before her. She is the embodiment of peace, knowledge, is praised by gods and grants every kind of wealth wished for.

> sakuṅkuma-vilepanāmalikacumbi-kastūrikāṃ
> samanda-hasitekṣaṇāṃ-saśara-cāpa-pāśāṅkuśām.
> aśeṣajana-mohinīṃ-aruṇa-mālya-bhūṣāmbarāṃ
> japākusuma-bhāsurāṃ-japavidhau-smare-dambikām..

I meditate upon the Mother, whose eyes are smiling, who holds the arrow, bow, noose and goad in her hands. She is glittering with red garlands and ornaments. She is painted with Kumkum on her forehead and is red and tender like the Japa flower.

Śhrī-mātā,Śhrī-mahā-rājñī,Śhrī-mat-simh'āsan'eśhvarī,
Chid-agni-kuṇḍa-sambhūtā,Deva-kārya-samudyatā. (1)

Udyad-bhānu-sahasrābhā,Chatur-bāhu-samanvitā,
Rāga-swarūpa-paśh'āḍhyā,Krodh'ākār'ānkuśh'ojjvalā. (2)

Mano-rūp'ekṣhu-kodaṇḍā,Pañcha-tanmātra-sāyakā,
Nij'āruṇa-prabhā-pūra-majjad-brahmāṇḍa-maṇḍalā. (3)

Champak'āśhoka-punnāga-saugandhika-lasat-kachā,
Kuruvinda-maṇi-śhreṇī-kanat-koṭīra-maṇḍitā. (4)

Aṣhṭamī-chandra-vibhrāja-dalika-sthala-śhobhitā,
Mukha-chandra-kalankābha-mṛiga-nābhi-viśheṣhakā. (5)

Vadana-smara-māngalya-gṛiha-toraṇa-chillikā,
Vaktra-lakshmi-parīvāha-chalan-mīn'ābha-lochanā. (6)

Nava-champaka-puṣhpābha-nāsā-ḍaṇḍa-virājitā,
Tārā-kānti-tiras-kāri-nāsā-bharaṇa-bhāsurā. (7)

Kadamba-mañjari-klṛipta-karṇa-pūra-manoharā,
Tāṭanka-yugalī-bhūta-tapan-oḍupa-maṇḍalā. (8)

Padma-rāga-śhil'ādarśha-pari-bhāvi-kapola-bhūḥ,
Nava-vidruma-bimba-śhrī-nyak-kāri-radanach-chhadā. (9)

Śhuddha-vidy'ānkur-ākāra-dvija-pankti-dvay'ojjvalā,
Karpūra-vīṭikā-moda-samākarṣhi-digantarā. (10)

Nija-sallāpa-mādhurya-vinir-bhartsita-kachchhapī,
Manda-smita-prabhāpūra-majjat-kāmeśha-mānasā. (11)

Anākalita-sādṛiśhya-chibuka-śhrī-virājitā,
Kāmeśha-baddha-māṅgalya-sūtra-śhobhita-kandharā. (12)

Kanak'āngada-keyūra-kamanīya-bhujānvitā,
Ratna-graiveya-chintāka-lola-muktā-phal'ānvitā. (13)

Kāmeśhwara-prema-ratna-maṇī-prati-paṇa-stanī,
Nābhy-ālavāla-romāli-latā-phala-kucha-dvayī. (14)

Lakṣhya-roma-latādhāra-ta-samunneya-madhyamā,
Stana-bhāra-dalan-madhya-paṭṭa-bandha-vali-trayā.(15)

Aruṇ'āruṇa-kausumbha-vastra-bhāswat-kaṭī-taṭī,
Ratna-kinkiṇikā-ramya-raśhanā-dāma-bhūṣhitā. (16)

Kāmeśha-gñyāta-saubhāgya-mārda-voru-dvay'ānvitā,
Māṇikya-mukuṭ'ākāra-jānu-dvaya-virājitā. (17)

Indra-gopa-parikṣhipta-smara-tūṇābha-jaṅghikā,
Gūḍha-gulphā-kūrma-pṛiṣhtha-jayiṣhṇu-prapad'ānvitā. (18)

Nakha-dīdhiti-samchhanna-namaj-jana-tamo-guṇā ,
Pada-dvaya-prabhājāla-parākṛita-saroruhā. (19)

Siñjāna-maṇi-mañjīra-maṇḍita-Śhrī-pad'āmbujā,
Marālī-manda-gamanā,Mahā-lāvaṇya-śhevadhiḥ. (20)

Sarv‘āruṇ‘ānavady‘āṅgī,Sarv‘ābharaṇa-bhūṣhitā,
Śhiva-kāmeśhwar‘āṅkasthā,Śhivā-Swādhīna-vallabhā. (21)

Sumeru-madhya-sṛiṅgha-sthā,Śhrīman-nagara-nāyikā,
Chintāmaṇi-gṛihānta-sthā,Pañcha-brahm‘āsana-sthitā. (22)

Mahā-padmāṭavi-samsthā,Kadamba-vana-vāsinī ,
Sudhā-sāgara-madhya-sthā,Kām‘ākṣhī-kāma-dāyinī. (23)

Devarṣhi-gaṇa-saṅghāta-stūya-mān’ātma-vaibhavā,
Bhaṇḍāsura-vadh‘odyukta-śhakti-senā-sam-anvitā. (24)

Sampat-karī-sam-ārūḍha-sindhura-vraja-sevitā ,
Aśhwārūḍh‘ādhi-ṣhṭhit‘āswa-koṭi-koṭibhir-āvṛitā. (25)

Chakra-rāja-rath‘ārūḍha-sarv‘āyudha-pariśh-kṛitā,
Geya-chakra-rath‘ārūḍha-mantriṇī-pari-sevitā. (26)

Kiri-chakra-rath‘ārūḍha-daṇḍa-nāthā-puraskṛitā,
Jvālā-mālini-kākṣhipta-vahni-prākāra-madhya-gā. (27)

Bhaṇḍa-sainyā-vadh‘od-yukta-śhaktī-vikrama-harṣhitā,
Nityā-par‘ākram‘āṭopa-nirīkṣhaṇa-sam-utsukā. (28)

Bhaṇḍa-putra-vadh‘od-yukta-bālā-vikrama-nanditā ,
Mantriṇy‘ambā-virachita-viṣhāṅga-vadha-toṣhitā. (29)

Viśhukra-prāṇa-haraṇa-vārāhī-vīrya-nanditā,
Kāmeśhwara-mukhāloka-kalpita-śhrī-gaṇeśhvarā. (30)

Mahā-gaṇesha-nirbhinna-vighna-yantra-praharṣhitā,
Bhaṇḍāsurendra-nirmukta-śhastra-pratyastra-varṣhiṇī. (31)

Kar'āṅguli-nakh'otpanna-nārāyaṇa-daśh'ākṛitiḥ,
Mahā-pāśhupat'āstrāgni-nirdagdh'āsura-sainikā. (32)

Kāmeśhvar'āstra-nirdagdha-sa-bhaṇḍāsura-śhūnyakā,
Brahm'opendra-mahendr'ādi-deva-samstuta-vaibhavā. (33)

Hara-netr'āgni-sam-dagdha-kāma-sañjīvan'auṣhadhiḥ,
Śhrīmad-vāg-bhava-kūṭaika-swarūpa-mukha-paṅkajā. (34)

Kaṇṭh'ādhaḥ-kaṭi-paryanta-madhya-kūṭa-swarūpiṇī,
Śhakti-kūṭaika-tāpanna-kaṭyadho-bhāga-dhariṇī. (35)

Mūla-mantr'ātmikā, Mūla-kūṭa-traya-kalebarā,
Kul'āmṛit'aika-rasika, Kula-saṅketa-pālinī. (36)

Kul'āṅganā, kul'ānta-sthā, Kaulinī, Kula-yoginī,
Akulā, Samay'ānta-sthā, Samay'āchāra-tatparā. (37)

Mūlādhār'aika-nilayā, Brahma-granthi-vibhedinī,
Maṇipur'āntar-uditā, Viṣhṇu-granthi-vibhedinī. (38)

Agñyā-chakr'āntarala-sthā, Rudra-granthi-vibhedinī,
Sahasrār'āmbuj'ārūḍhā, Sudhā-sār'ābhi-varṣhiṇī. (39)

Taḍillata-sama-ruchiḥ, ṣhat-chakr'opari-samsthitā,
Mahā-śhaktiḥ, Kuṇḍalinī, Bisa-tantu-tanīyasī. (40)

Bhavānī, Bhāvan'āgamyā, Bhav'āraṇya-kuṭhārikā,
Bhadra-priyā, Bhadra-mūrtir, Bhaktā-saubhāgya-dāyinī. (41)

Bhakti-priyā, Bhakti-gamyā, Bhakti-vaśhyā, Bhay'āpahā,
Śhāmbhavī, Śhārad'ārādhyā, Śharvaṇī, Śharma-dāyinī. (42)

Śham-karī, Śhrī-karī, Sādhvī, Śharach-chandra-nibh'ānanā,
Śhāt-odarī, Śhānti-matī, Nir-ādhārā, Nir-añjanā. (43)

Nirlepā, Nirmalā, Nityā, Nir-ākārā, Nir-ākulā ,
Nirguṇā, Niṣhkalā, Śhāntā, Niṣhkāmā, Nir-upaplavā. (44)

Nitya-muktā, Nir-vikarā, Niṣh-prapañchā, Nir-āśhrayā,
Nitya-śhuddhā, Nitya-buddhā, Nir-avadyā, Nir-antarā. (45)

Niṣh-kāraṇā, Niṣh-kalaṅkā, Nir-upādhir, Nir-īśhwarā,
Nīrāgā, Rāga-mathanī, Nirmadā, Mada-nāśhinī. (46)

Nischintā, Nir-ahaṁkarā, Nir-mohā, Moha-nāśhinī,
Nirmamā, Mamatā-hantrī, Niṣhpāpā, Pāpa-nāśhinī. (47)

Niṣh-krodhā, Krodha-śhamanī, Nir-lobhā, Lobha-nāśhinī,
Niḥ-samśhayā, Samśhaya-ghnī, Nir-bhavā, Bhava-nāśhinī. (48)

Nir-vikalpā, Nir-ābādhā, Nirbhedā, Bheda-nāśhinī ,
Nir-nāśhā, Mṛityu-mathanī, Niṣhkriyā, Niṣh-parigrahā. (49)

Nistulā, Nīla-chikurā, Nirapāyā, Niratyayā,
Dur-labhā, Dur-gamā, Durgā, Duḥkhahantrī, Sukhapradā. (50)

Dushta-dūrā,Dur-āchāra-śhamanī,Dosha-varjitā,
Sarva-gñyā,Sāndra-karuṇā,Samānādhika-varjitā. (51)

Sarva-śhakti-mayī,Sarva-māṅgalā,Sad-gati-pradā,
Sarveśhwarī,Sarva-mayī,Sarva-mantra-swarūpiṇī. (52)

Sarva-yantr-ātmikā,Sarva-tantra-rūpā,Man'on-manī,
Maheśhwarī,Mahādevī,Mahā-lakṣhmī,Mṛiḍa-priyā. (53)

Mahā-rūpā,Mahā-pūjyā,Mahā-pātaka-nāśhinī,
Mahā-māyā,Mahā-sattwā,Mahā-śhaktir,Mahā-ratiḥ. (54)

Mahā-bhogā,Mah'aiswaryā,Mahā-viryā,Mahā-balā,
Mahā-buddhir,Mahā-siddhir,Mahā-yogeśhwar'eśhwarī. (55)

Mahā-tantrā,Mahā-mantrā,Mahā-yantrā,Mahāsanā,
Mahā-yaga-kram'ārādhyā,Mahā-bhairava-pūjitā. (56)

Maheśhvara-mahā-kalpa-mahā-tāṇḍava-sākṣhiṇī,
Mahā-kāmeśha-mahiṣhī,Mahā-tripura-sundarī. (57)

Chatuḥ-ṣhaṣhṭy'upa-chārāḍhyā,Chatuḥ-ṣhaṣhṭi-kalā-mayī,
Mahā-chatuḥ-ṣhaṣhti-koṭi-yoginī-gaṇa-sevitā. (58)

Manu-vidyā,Chandra-vidyā,Chandra-maṇḍala-madhya-gā,
Chāru-rūpā,Chāru-hāsā,Chāru-chandra-kalā-dharā. (59)

Char'āchara-jagan-nāthā,Chakra-rāja-niketanā,
Pārvatī,Padma-nayanā,Padma-rāga-sama-prabhā. (60)

Pañcha-pret'āsan-āsīnā, Pañcha-brahma-swarūpiṇī,
Chin-mayī, Param-ānandā, Vigñyāna-ghana-rūpiṇī. (61)

Dhyāna-dhyātṛi-dhyeya-rūpā, Dharm'ādharma-vivarjitā,
Vishwa-rūpā, Jāgariṇī, Swapantī, Taijas-ātmikā. (62)

Suptā, Prāgñy'ātmikā, Turyā, Sarv'āvasthā-vivarjitā,
Sṛiṣhṭi-kartrī, Brahma-rūpā, Goptrī, Govinda-rūpiṇī. (63)

Saṁhāriṇī, Rudra-rūpā, Tirodhāna-karī, Īśhvarī,
Sadā-śhiva, 'Ānu-graha-dā, Pañcha-kṛitya-parāyaṇā. (64)

Bhānu-maṇḍala-madhya-sthā, Bhairavī, Bhaga-mālinī,
Padmāsanā, Bhagavatī, Padma-nābha-sahodarī. (65)

Unmeṣha-nimiṣh'otpanna-vipanna-bhuvan'āvalī,
Sahasra-śhīrṣha-vadanā, Sahasr'ākṣhī, Sahasra-pāt. (66)

Ā-brahma-kiṭa-jananī, Varṇ'āśhrama-vidhāyinī ,
Nij'āgñyā-rūpa-nigamā, Puṇy'āpuṇya-phala-pradā.(67)

Śhruti-sīmanta-sindūrī-kṛita-pādābja-dhūlikā,
Sakal'āgama-saṁdoha-śhukti-saṁpuṭa-mauktikā. (68)

Puruṣh'ārtha-pradā, Pūrṇā, Bhoginī, Bhuvaneśhvarī,
Ambik'ānādi-nidhanā, Hari-brahm'endra-sevitā. (69)

Nārāyaṇī, nāda-rūpā, Nāma-rūpa-vivarjitā,
Hrīṁ-kārī, Hrīṁ-matī, Hṛidyā, Heyopādeya-varjitā. (70)

Rāja-rāj'ārchitā,Rājñī,Ramyā,Rājīva-lochanā,
Rañjanī,Ramaṇī,Rasyā,Raṇat-kiṅkiṇi-mekhalā. (71)

Ramā,Rākendu-vadanā,Rati-rūpā,Rati-priyā ,
Rakṣhā-karī,Rākṣhasa-ghnī,Rāmā,Ramaṇa-lampaṭā. (72)

Kāmyā,Kāma-kalā-rūpā,Kadamba-kusuma-priyā,
Kalyāṇī,Jagatī-kandā,Karuṇā-rasa-sāgarā. (73)

Kalā-vatī,Kal'ālāpā,Kāntā,Kādambarī-priyā,
Varadā,Vāma-nayanā,Vāruṇī-mada-vihvalā. (74)

Viśhw'ādhikā,Veda-vedyā,Vindhy'āchala-nivāsinī,
Vidhātrī,Veda-jananī,Viṣhṇu-māyā,Vilāsinī. (75)

Kṣhetra-swarūpā,Kṣhetreśhī,Kṣhetra-kṣhetra-gñya-pālinī,
Kṣhaya-vṛiddhi-vinir-muktā,Kṣhetra-pāla-sam-architā. (76)

Vijayā,Vimalā,Vandyā,Vandāru-jana-vatsalā ,
Vāg-vādinī,Vāmakeśhī,Vahni-maṇḍala-vāsinī. (77)

Bhakti-mat-kalpa-latikā,Paśhu-pāśha-vimochinī,
Saṁ-hṛit'āśheṣha-pāṣhaṇḍā,Sad-āchāra-pra-vartikā. (78)

Tāpa-tray'āgni-samtapta-samāhlādana-chandrikā,
Taruṇī,Tāpas'ārādhyā,Tanu-madhyā,Tamō'pahā. (79)

Chitih,Tat-pada-lakṣhy'ārthā,Chid-eka-rasa-rūpiṇī ,
Swātm'ānanda-lavī-bhūta-brahm'ādy'ānanda-santatiḥ. (80)

Parā,Pratyak-chitī-rūpā,Paśhyantī,Paradevatā,
Madhyamā,Vaikharī-rūpā,Bhakta-mānasa-hamsikā. (81)

Kāmeśhvara-prāṇa-nāḍī,Kṛita-gñyā Kāma-pūjitā,
Śhṛiṅgāra-rasa-sampūrṇā,Jayā,Jālan-dhara-sthitā. (82)

Oḍyāṇa-pīṭha-nilayā,Bindu-maṇḍala-vāsinī,
Rahoyāga-kram'ārādhyā,Rahas-tarpaṇa-tarpitā. (83)

Sadyah-prasādinī,Vīśhva-sākṣhiṇī,Sākṣhi-varjitā,
Ṣhaḍ-aṅga-devatā-yuktā,ṣhāḍ-guṇya-pari-pūritā. (84)

Nitya-klinnā,Nir-upamā,Nirvāṇa-sukha-dāyinī,
Nityā-ṣhoḍaśhikā-rūpā,Śhrī-kaṇṭh'ārdha-śharīriṇī. (85)

Prabhāvatī,Prabhā-rūpā,Prasiddhā,Parameśhvarī,
Mūla-prakṛitiḥ,Avyaktā,Vyakt'āvyakta-swarūpiṇī. (86)

Vyāpinī,Vividh'ākārā,Vidy'āvidyā-swarūpiṇī,
Mahākāmeśha-nayana-kumud'āhlāda-kaumudī. (87)

Bhakta-hārda-tamo-bheda-bhānu-mad-bhānu-saṇtatiḥ,
Śhiva-dūtī,Śhiv'ārādhyā,Śhiva-mūrtiḥ,Śhivam-karī. (88)

Śhiva-priyā,Śhiva-parā,Śhiṣhteṣhtā,Śhiṣhta-pūjitā,
Aprameyā,Swa-prakāśhā,Mano-vāchām-agocharā. (89)

Chit-śhaktiśh,Chetana-rūpā,Jaḍa-śhaktir,Jaḍ'ātmikā,
Gāyatrī,Vyāhṛitiḥ,Sandhyā,Dvija-vṛinda-niṣhevitā. (90)

Tattw'āsanā,Tat,Twam,Ayī,Pañcha-koṣh'āntara-sthitā,
Niḥ-sīma-mahimā,Nitya-yauvanā,Mada-śhālinī. (91)

Mada-ghūrṇita-rakt'ākṣhī,Mada-pāṭala-gaṇḍa-bhūḥ ,
Chandana-drava-digdh'āṅgī,Chāmpeya-kusuma-priyā. (92)

Kuśhalā,Komal'ākārā,Kurukullā,Kuleśhvarī,
Kula-kuṇḍālayā,Kaula-mārga-tatpara-sevitā. (93)

Kumāra-gaṇa-nāth'āmbā,Tuṣhṭiḥ,Puṣhṭir,Matir,Dhṛitiḥ,
Śhāntiḥ,Swasti-matī,kāntir,Nandinī,Vighna-nāśhinī. (94)

Tejovatī,Tri-nayanā,Lolākṣhī,Kāma-rūpiṇī,
Mālinī,Hamsinī,Mātā,Malay'āchala-vāsinī. (95)

Su-mukhī,Nalinī,Su-bhrūḥ,Śhobhanā,Sura-nāyikā,
Kāla-kaṇṭhī,Kānti-matī,Kṣhobhiṇī,Sūkṣhma-rūpiṇī. (96)

Vajreśhvarī,Vāma-devī,Vayō'vasthā-vivarjita,
Siddheśhvarī,Siddha-vidyā,Siddha-mātā,Yaśhaswinī. (97)

Viśhuddhi-chakra-nilaya,"Rakta-varṇā,Tri-lochanā,
Khaṭvāṅg'ādi-pra-haraṇā,Vadan'aika-samanvitā. (98)

Pāyas'ānna-priyā,Tvak-sthā,Paśhu-loka-bhayañ-karī,
Amṛit'ādi-mahāśhakti-samvṛitā,Ḍākin'īśhwarī. (99)

Anāhat'ābja-nilayā,Śhyām'ābhā,Vadana-dvayā,
Danṣhṭrojjvalā,Akṣhamālādi-dharā,Rudhira-samsthitā. (100)

Kāla-rātry'Ādi-shakty'Augha-vṛitā,Snigdh'audana-priyā,
Mahā-vīrendra-varadā,Rākiṇy'ambā-swarūpiṇī. (101)

Maṇipūr'ābja-nilayā,Vadana-traya-samyutā,
Vajr'ādik'āyudh-opetā,Ḍāmary'ādi-bhir-āvṛitā. (102)

Rakta-varṇā,Mamsa-niṣhṭhā,Guḍ'ānna-prīta-mānasā,
Samasta-bhakta-sukhadā,Lākiny'ambā-swarūpiṇī. (103)

Swādhiṣhṭhān'āmbuja-gatā,Chatur-vaktra-manoharā,
Śhūlādy'āyudha-sampannā,Pīta-varna,Āti-garvitā. (104)

Medo-niṣhṭhā,Madhu-prītā,Bandhiny'ādi-samanvitā,
Dadhyann'āsakta-hṛidayā,Kākinī-rūpa-dhāriṇī. (105)

Mūlādhār'āmbuj'ārūḍhā,Pañcha-vaktra,'Āsthi-samsthitā,
Aṅkuśh'ādi-praharaṇā,Varad'ādi-niṣhevitā. (106)

Mudgaudan'āsakta-chittā,Sākiny'ambā-swarūpiṇī,
Āgñyā-chakr'ābja-nilayā,Śhukla-varṇā,Ṣhad-ananā. (107)

Majjā-samsthā,Haṁsavatī-mukhya-śhakti-samanvitā,
Haridr'ānn'aika-rasikā,Hākinī-rūpa-dhāriṇī. (108)

Sahasra-dala-padma-sthā,Sarva-varṇ'opa-śhobhitā,
Sarv'āyudha-dharā,Śhukla-sam-sthitā,Sarvato-mukhī. (109)

Sarv'audana-prīta-chittā,Yakiny'amba-swarūpiṇī,
Swāhā,Swadhā,MatirMedhā,Śhrutiḥ,Smṛitir,Anuttamā.(110)

Puṇya-kīrtiḥ,Puṇya-labhyā,Puṇya-śhravaṇa-kīrtanā,
Pulomaj'ārchitā,Bandha-mochanī,Bandhur'ālakā. (111)

Vimarśha-rūpiṇī,Vidyā,Viyad-ādi-jagat-prasūḥ,
Sarva-vyādhi-praśhamanī,Sarva-mṛityu-nivāriṇī. (112)

Agra-gaṇya,'Āchintya-rūpā,Kali-kalmaṣha-nāśhinī,
Kātyāyanī,Kāla-hantrī,Kamal'ākṣha-niṣhevitā. (113)

Tāmbūla-pūrita-mukhī,Dāḍimī-kusuma-prabhā,
Mṛig'ākṣhī,Mohinī,Mukhyā,Mṛiḍānī,Mitra-rūpiṇī. (114)

Nitya-tṛiptā,Bhakta-nidhir,Niyantrī,Nikhil'eśhvarī,
Maitry'ādi-vāsanā-labhyā,Mahā-pralaya-sākṣhiṇī. (115)

Parā-śhaktiḥ,Parā-niṣhṭhā,Pra-gñyāna-ghana-rūpiṇī,
Mādhvī-pānālasā,Mattā,Matṛika-varṇa-rūpiṇī. (116)

Mahā-kailāsa-nilayā,Mṛiṇāla-mridu-dorlatā,
Mahanīyā,Dayā-mūrtir,Mahā-sām-rājya-śhālinī. (117)

Ātma-vidyā,Mahā-vidyā,Śhrī-vidyā,Kāma-sevitā ,
Śhrī-ṣhoḍaśh'ākṣharī-vidyā,Trikūṭā,Kāma-koṭikā. (118)

Kaṭākṣha-kiṁkarī-bhūta-kamalā-koṭi-sevitā,
Śhiraḥsthitā,Chandranibhā,Bhālasthendra-dhanuṣh-prabhā.
(119)

Hṛidaya-sthā,Ravi-prakhyā,Trikoṇ'āntara-dīpikā,
Dākṣhāyaṇī,Daitya-hantrī,Dakṣha-yagñya-vināśhinī. (120)

Darāndolita-dīrgh'ākṣhī,Dara-hās'oj-jvalan-mukhī,
Guru-mūrtir,Guṇa-nidhir,Gomātā,Guha-janma-bhūḥ. (121)

Deveśhī,Daṇḍa-nītisthā,Dahar'ākāśha-rūpiṇī,
Pratipan-mukhya-rākānta-tithi-maṇḍala-pūjita. (122)

Kal'ātmikā,Kalā-nāthā,Kāvy'ālāpa-vinodinī,
Sa-chāmara-ramā-vāṇī-savya-dakṣhiṇa-sevitā. (123)

Ādi-śhaktiḥ,Amey'ātmā,Paramā Pāvan'ākṛitiḥ,
Aneka-koṭi-brahmāṇḍa-jananī,Divya-vigrahā. (124)

Klīṁ-kārī,Kevalā,Guhyā,Kaivalya-pada-dāyinī,
Tripurā,Tri-jagad-vandyā,Tri-mūrtir,Tri-daśh'eśhvarī. (125)

Try'akṣharī,Divya-gandh'āḍhyā,Sindūra-tilak'ānchitā,
Umā,Śhailendra-tanayā,Gaurī,Gandharva-sevitā. (126)

Viśhva-garbhā,Svarṇa-garbhā,Varadā,Vāg-adhīśhvarī,
Dhyāna-gamyā,Aparichchhedyā,Gñyānadā,Gñyāna-vigrahā.
(127)

Sarva-vedānta-saṁ-vedyā,Saty'ānanda-sva-rūpiṇī,
Lopāmudr'ārchitā,Līlā-klṛipta-brahmāṇḍa-maṇḍalā. (128)

Adṛiśhyā,Dṛiśhya-rahitā,Vigñyātrī,Vedya-varjitā,
Yoginī,Yoga-dā,Yogyā,Yog'ānandā,Yugan-dharā. (129)

Ichchhā-śhaktī-gñyānā-śhaktī-krīya-śhaktī-sva-rūpiṇī,
Sarv'ādhārā,Su-pratiṣhṭhā,Sad-asad-rūpa-dhārinī. (130)

Aṣhṭa-mūrtir,Ajā,Jetrī,Loka-yātrā-vidhāyinī,
Ekākinī,Bhūma-rūpā,Nir-dvaitā,Dvaita-varjitā. (131)

Anna-dā,Vasu-dā,Vṛiddhā,Brahm'ātmaikya-sva-rūpiṇī,
Bṛihatī,Brāhmaṇī,Brahmī,Brahm'ānandā,Bali-priyā. (132)

Bhāṣhā-rūpā,Bṛihat-senā,Bhāv'ābhāva-vivarjitā,
Sukh'ārādhyā,Shubha-karī,Shobhanā-sulabh'āgatiḥ. (133)

Rāja-rājeshvarī,Rājya-dāyinī,Rājya-vallabhā,
Rājat-kṛipā,Rāja-pīṭha-niveshita-nij'āshritā. (134)

Rājya-lakshmīḥ,Kosha-nāthā,Chatur-aṅga-baleshvarī,
Sām-rājya-dāyinī,Satya-sandhā,Sāgara-mekhalā. (135)

Dīkṣhitā,Daitya-shamanī,Sarva-loka-vasham-karī,
Sarvārtha-dātrī,Sāvitrī,Sach-chid-ānanda-rūpiṇī. (136)

Desha-kāl'āparich-chhinnā,Sarva-gā,Sarva-mohinī,
Saraswatī,Shāstra-mayī,Guhāmbā,Guhya-rūpiṇī. (137)

Sarv'opādhi-vinir-muktā,Sadāshiva-pati-vratā,
Sam-pra-dāyeshvarī,Sādhu,Ī,Guru-maṇḍala-rūpiṇī. (138)

Kulot-tīrṇā,Bhag'ārādhyā,Māyā,Madhu-matī,Mahī,
Gaṇāmbā,Guhyak'ārādhyā,Komal'aṅgī,Guru-priyā. (139)

Swa-tantrā,Sarva-tantreshī,Dakṣhīṇā-mūrti-rūpiṇī,
Sanak'ādi-sam-ārādhyā,Shiva-gñyāna-pradāyinī. (140)

Chit-kalā,'Ananda-kalikā,Prema-rūpā,Priyaṁ-karī,
Nāma-pārāyaṇa-prītā,Nandi-vidyā,Naṭeśhvarī. (141)

Mithyā-jagad-adhi-ṣhṭhānā,Mukti-dā,Mukti-rūpiṇī,
Lāsya-priyā,Laya-karī,Lajjā,Rambh'ādi-vanditā. (142)

Bhava-dāva-sudha-vṛiṣhtiḥ,Pāp'ārāṇya-davānalā ,
Daur-bhāgya-tūla-vātūlā,Jarādhv'āntara-viprabhā. (143)

Bhāgyābdhi-chandrikā,Bhakta-chitta-keki-ghan'āghanā,
Roga-parvata-dambholir,Mṛityu-dāru-kuṭhārikā. (144)

Maheśhvarī,Mahā-kālī,Mahā-grasā,Mahā-śhanā,
Aparṇā,Chaṇḍikā,Chaṇḍa-muṇḍ'āsura-niṣhūdinī. (145)

Kṣhar'ākṣhar'ātmikā,Sarva-lokeśhī,Viśhva-dhāriṇī,
Tri-varga-dātrī,Su-bhagā,Try'ambakā,Tri-guṇ'ātmikā. (146)

Swarg'āpa-varga-dā,Śhuddhā,Japā-puṣhpa-nibh'ākṛitiḥ,
Ojovatī,Dyuti-dharā,Yagñya-rūpā,Priya-vratā. (147)

Dur-ārādhyā,Dur-ādharṣhā,Pāṭali-kusuma-priyā,
Mahatī,Meru-nilayā,Mandāra-kusuma-priyā. (148)

Vīr'ārādhyā,Virāḍ-rūpā,Vi-rajā,Viśhwato-mukhī,
Pratyag-rūpā,Par'ākāśhā,Prāṇa-dā,Prāṇa-rūpinī. (149)

Mārtaṇḍa-bhairav'ārādhyā,Mantriṇī-nyasta-rājya-dhūḥ,
Tri-pureśhī,jayat-senā,Nis-trai-guṇyā,Par'āparā. (150)

Satya-gñyān'ānanda-rūpā,Sāmarasya-parāyaṇā,
Kapardinī,kalā-mālā,Kāma-dhuk,Kāma-rūpiṇī.(151)

Kalā-nidhiḥ,Kāvya-kalā,Rasa-gñyā,Rasa-śhevadhiḥ,
Puṣhṭā,Purātanā,Pūjyā,Puṣhkarā,Puṣhkar'ekṣhaṇā. (152)

Param-jyotiḥ,Param-dhāmā,Param-āṇuḥ,Parāt-parā,
Pāśha-hastā,Pāśha-hantrī,Para-mantra-vibhedinī. (153)

Mūrtā,Āmūrtā,Anitya-tṛiptā,Muni-mānasa-hamsikā,
Satya-vratā,Satya-rūpā,Sarv'āntar-yāminī,Satī. (154)

Brahmāṇī,Brahma,Jananī,Bahu-rūpā,Budh'ārchitā,
Prasavitrī,Prachaṇd'āgñyā,Pratiṣhṭhā,Prakaṭ'ākṛitiḥ. (155)

Prāṇeśhvarī,Prāṇa-dātrī,Pañchāśhat-pīṭha-rūpiṇī,
Viśhṛiṇ-khalā,Vivikta-sthā,Vīra-mātā,Viyat-prasūḥ. (156)

Mukundā,Mukti-nilayā,Mūla-vigraha-rūpiṇī,
Bhāva-gñyā,Bhava-roga-ghnī,Bhava-chakra-pravartinī. (157)

Chhandaḥ-sārā,Śhāstra-sārā,Mantra-sārā,Talodarī,
Udāra-kīrtir,Uddāma-vaibhavā,Varṇa-rūpiṇī. (158)

Janma-mṛityu-jarā-tapta-jana-viśhrānti-dāyinī,
Sarv'opaniṣhad-ud-ghuṣhṭā,Śhānty'atīta-kal'ātmikā. (159)

Gambhīrā,Gagan'ānta-sthā,Garvitā,Gāna-lolupā,
Kalpanā-rahitā,Kāṣhṭhā,'AKāntā,Kānt'ardha-vigrahā. (160)

Kārya-kāraṇa-nir-muktā,Kāma-keli-tarañ-gitā,
Kanat-kanaka-tāṭankā,Līlā-vigraha-dhāriṇī. (161)

Aja,kṣhaya-vinir-muktā,Mugdhā,Kṣhipra-prasādinī,
Antar-mukha-samārādhyā,Bahir-mukha-su-dur-labhā. (162)

Trayī,Trivarga-nilayā,Tri-sthā,Tripura-mālinī,
Nir-āmayā,Nir-ālambā,Sw'ātmā-rāmā,Sudhā-sṛutiḥ. (163)

Saṁsāra-panka-nir-magna-sam-uddharaṇa-paṇditā,
Yagñya-priyā,Yagñya-kartrī,Yajamāna-swarūpiṇī. (164)

Dharm'ādhārā,Dhan'ādhyakṣhā,Dhana-dhānya-vivardhinī,
Vipra-priyā,Vipra-rūpā,Viśhwa-bhramaṇa-kāriṇī. (165)

Viśhwa-grāsā,Vidrum-ābhā,Vaiṣhṇavī,Viṣhṇu-rūpiṇī,
Ayoniḥ,Yoni-nilayā,Kūṭa-sthā,Kula-rūpiṇī. (166)

Vīra-goṣhṭhī-priya,Vīrā,Naiṣh-karmyā,Nāda-rūpiṇī ,
Vigñyāna-kalanā,Kalyā,Vidagdhā,Baindav-āsanā. (167)

Tattw'ādhikā,Tattwa-mayī,Tattwam-artha-rūpinī,
Sāma-gāna-priyā,Saumyā,Sadāśhiva-kuṭumbinī. (168)

Savy'āpa-savya-mārga-sthā,Sarvāpad-vini-vāriṇī,
Swasthā,Swabhāva-madhurā,Dhirā,Dhira-sam-architā. (169)

Chaitany-ārghya-sam-ārādhyā,Chaitanya-kusuma-priyā,
Sadoditā,Sadātuṣhṭā,Taruṇ-āditya-pāṭalā. (170)

Dakṣhiṇ'ādakṣhiṇ'ārādhyā,Dara-smera-mukh'āmbujā,
Kaulinī-kevalā,'Anardhya-kaivalya-pada-dāyinī. (171)

Stotra-priyā,Stuti-matī,Śhruti-saṁ-stuta-vaibhavā,
Manasvinī,Māna-vatī,Maheśhī,Maṅgal'ākṛitiḥ. (172)

Viśhwa-mātā,Jagad-dhātrī,Viśhāl'ākṣhī,Vi-rāgiṇī,
Pra-galbhā,Param'odārā,Par'āmodā,Mano-mayī. (173)

Vyoma-keśhī,Vimāna-sthā,Vajriṇī,Vāmak'eśhvarī,
Pañchayagñya-priyā,Pañchapreta-mañch'ādhi-śhāyinī. (174)

Paṇchamī,Pañcha-bhūteśhī,Pañcha-saṁkhy'opa-chārinī,
Śhāśhwatī,Śhāśhwat'aiśhwaryā,Śharmadā,Śhambhu-mohinī.
(175)

Dharā,Dhara-sutā,Dhanyā,Dharmiṇī,Dharma-vardhinī,
Lok'ātītā,Guṇ'ātītā,Sarv'ātītā,Śham'ātmikā. (176)

Bandhūka-kusuma-prakhyā,Bālā,Līla-vinodinī,
Su-maṅgalī,Sukha-karī,Suveṣh-āḍhyā,Su-vāsinī. (177)

Su-vāsiny-archana-prītā,Āshobhanā,Śhuddha-mānasā,
Bindu-tarpaṇa-santuṣhṭā,Pūrva-jā,Tri-pur'āmbikā. (178)

Daśha-mudra-sam-ārādhyā,Tripurā-śhrī-vaśham-karī,
Gñyānamudrā,Gñyānagamyā,Gñyānagñyeyasvarūpiṇī. (179)

Yoni-mudrā,Tri-khaṇḍeśhī,Tri-guṇā,Ambā,Trikoṇa-gā,
Anaghā,Adbhuta-chāritrā,Vāñchhit'ārtha-pradāyinī. (180)

Abhyās'ātiśhaya-gñyātā,Ṣhaḍ-adhv'ātīta-rūpiṇī,
Avyāja-karuṇā-mūrtir,Agñyāna-dhvānta-dīpikā. (181)

Ābāla-gopa-viditā,Sarv'ān-ullaṅghya-śhāsanā,
Śhrī-chakra-rāja-nilayā,Śhrīmat-tripura-sundarī. (182)

Śhrī-śhivā-Śhiva-śhakty'aikya-rūpiṇī-Lalit'āmbikā. (183)

All hail, Divine Mother! You embody the sacred union of Shiva and Shakti, the very essence of Oneness. From you, O Lalita, flows the entire universe, a magnificent play of your divine will.

Here ends the Thousand Names of Shri Lalita as a poem.

Think Deeper: Essential Prompts and Insights

— ✳ —

Lalita Devi: Unveiling the Divine Within

The Verses 1-23 delves into the interconnectedness of the human body, mind, senses and the universe, using captivating descriptions of the body and its flawless nature. It emphasizes that every part of our physical form works in perfect harmony, highlighting the wonder and complexity of existence. Within these 23 verses, the object of worship is not any idol/photo of Lalitambika; rather, it is the manifestation of our own being.

These verses transcends mere physical beauty by stating that the universe itself is our adornment, with countless stars and planets reflecting the grand scale of our existence. It emphasizes the concept of microcosm and macrocosm: that we, as individuals, are miniature reflections of the vast cosmos.

Furthermore, the verses introduce the concept of **SHIVOHAM,** which translates to "I am Shiva." This echoes the idea that the divine essence, Sri-Siva, resides within each of us. This connects the concept to the **NAMAH SHIVAYA** mantra, which is associated with the Panchamahabhutas (five elements) – earth, water, fire, air, and space. Lalita Sahasranama takes us from **NAMAH SHIVAYA** mantra to **SHIVOHAM.** The Shakti is the dynamic energy in us. This interplay between static and dynamic states of energy is crucial for existence.

While the verses describes the individual body as flawless, it goes beyond this physical beauty and unveils a deeper spiritual meaning. It explains that Shiva, representing the unchanging aspect of reality, needs the dynamic energy of Shakti to manifest and create the universe.

Concluding with a reference to Lalitambika, the last verse of the Lalita Sahasranama - **"Śhrī-śhivā-Śhiva-śhakty'aikya-rūpiṇī-Lalit'āmbikā"** - **(Verse 183)** - the verse underscores the unity of Shiva and Shakti. It emphasizes that Lalitambika embodies the oneness of these divine forces, and her playful interaction forms the very essence of our universe.

Overall, this verse delves into spiritual concepts using evocative imagery and poetic language. It highlights the interconnectedness of the human body, the universe, and the divine.

Sri Yantra and the Human Connection

Glory to the radiant goddess who is residing on the middle peak of Mount Meru, who is the Queen of the Auspicious City, Occupying the mansion of wish-fulfilling gems, on a couch of the five aspects of God. **(Verse 22)**

The central dot (bindu) in the Sri Yantra symbolizes the perfect union of Shiva and Shakti, the divine masculine and feminine energies. Within the human body, this dot corresponds to the crown of the head - Crown Chakra, a sacred center of spiritual awareness.

The term **"Sumeru"** has a dual meaning: it represents both the devotee's body or backbone, as well as the three-dimensional form of the Sri Yantra known as **"Meru Prastara"**.

Lalita Devi is depicted seated on a throne supported by four deities: Brahma, Vishnu, Rudra, and Ishvara. These gods symbolize the four aspects of creation, preservation, destruction, and concealment. The central plank of the throne is Sadasiva, representing the foundation of pure consciousness. This reveals how the supreme power of the divine rests upon these fundamental elements that govern the natural world.

Similarly, the human body is a vessel created from the five elements - earth, water, fire, air and space. These elements reside within the various chakras (energy centers) along the spine, from the muladhara (root) to the visuddhi (throat), governing their respective functions within the body. This structure formed by the chakras is known as the 'throne of five gods', highlighting the deep connection between the human body and the cosmic structure.

Verses on the Battlefield

Chanting the verses on the battlefield brings a profound sense of inner peace.

The Verses 24 to 33 describes the battle between Lalita Devi and Bhandasura, a demon representing ignorance, ego, and resulting negativity. Let's delve into the deeper meaning of this symbolic battle:

The word **"Bhanda"** means shameless, while **"Asura"** translates to demon. Put together, Bhandasura represents the shameless demon, symbolizing the lack of moral compass and ethical boundaries fueled by ignorance and ego.

This battle isn't a physical one but a symbolic representation of the internal struggle within each individual. Bhandasura embodies the negative aspects we all encounter within ourselves. **Vishanga:** This word signifies the infatuation of the senses with external objects. Defeating Vishanga represents turning our attention inwards, away from external distractions, and towards meditation and self-awareness. This is akin to the yogic practice of pratyahara, or withdrawal of the senses. **Vishukra:** This term refers to negative energies. Conquering Vishukra signifies overcoming negativity within our minds, which can manifest as uncontrolled desires, anger, and hatred. The Bhandasura sons represent the detrimental habits that arise from these internal conflicts.

Lalita Devi's Divine Army:

Lalita Devi's army isn't composed of physical soldiers but represents the divine qualities nurtured within a devotee during their spiritual journey. Blooming Virtues: The army preparing for battle signifies the development of these virtues within the individual, such as compassion, courage, and self-discipline. Divine Forms: Lalita Devi herself embodies different aspects of these virtues through her forms like Sampathkari, Ashva-Rudha, Mantrini, Bala, Varahi, Jwala-Malini and Ganesha. These forms empower the devotee and provide them with various tools to overcome negativity.

Overall, the battle between Lalita Devi and Bhandasura symbolizes the ongoing internal struggle between negativity and the cultivation of positive qualities. Lalita Devi represents the divine spark within each individual, guiding us towards self- realization and liberation.

The verses mentions the process of uprooting samskaras, negative impressions from this life and past lives. This is often described as a painful process, hence the association with the "punishing goddess" Varahi, a form of Lalita Devi. The concept of subconscious programming emphasizes the importance of addressing negativity on a deeper level beyond just conscious thought.

Remember, this is just one interpretation of the symbolism. The beauty of spiritual stories lies in their ability to offer various layers of meaning and personal reflection for each individual.

The Story of Sati and Daksha: The Importance of Divine Connection

In the heart, You are effulgent like the sun, You are the flame inside the Triangle of Muladhar; You are Shri Sati - the Daughter of Daksha and First Wife of Lord Shiva, the Slayer of the demons, and the Destroyer of King Daksha's sacrifice. **(Verse 120)**

In the rich tapestry of Indian mythology, we find the story of Sati, daughter of the powerful King Daksha. Sati, also known as Dakshayini, represents the embodiment of the Divine Mother. Despite her divine lineage, Daksha harbored a deep resentment for Lord Shiva, Sati's husband.

Driven by pride, Daksha held a grand fire ritual, deliberately excluding Lord Shiva. This act of disrespect severed the vital connection to the Divine. Without his sacred presence, the ritual descended into chaos, becoming a breeding ground for negativity.

Overwhelmed with grief and recognizing the tainted nature of the ritual, Sati sacrificed herself in the flames. Blinded by rage at this immense loss, Lord Shiva unleashed a powerful force, Veerabhadra, who in turn brought about the destruction of Daksha and the ritual itself. While Veerabhadra was the instrument of destruction, the root cause lay in Daksha's severed connection with the Divine.

This story conveys a profound message: any action, no matter how grand, risks futility and even ruin if it disregards the divine. It highlights the importance of inviting sacred energy into our endeavors and maintaining a constant awareness of something greater than ourselves. It invites us to reflect on the significance of our connection with life and a higher power.

Six Paths of Devotion

Glory to the Divine Mother - In meditation, your divine form reveals itself, O Mother. You stand at the culmination of devotion's six paths, embodying selfless love. Like a radiant lamp, you banish the darkness of ignorance. **(Verse 181)**

The six paths of devotion, also known as the **Shattvika Bhakti Margas** are:

Shraddha (Faith): This path emphasizes complete trust and surrender to the divine. It's about having a deep conviction in the existence and power of a higher force.

Bhakti (Devotion): This path focuses on cultivating pure love and devotion towards the divine. It's about developing a deep emotional connection with the Divine Mother.

Smarana (Remembering): This path involves constantly keeping the divine in your mind through mantras, prayers, and meditation. It's about staying connected to the Divine Mother through continuous remembrance.

Seva (Service): This path emphasizes selfless service to the divine, often through acts of charity or helping others. It's about expressing devotion through actions that benefit others.

Saakhyam (Knowledge): This path emphasizes gaining true spiritual knowledge through scriptures, teachers, and personal reflection. It's about understanding the divine and your place in the universe.

Samadhi (Surrender): This path is the ultimate state of devotion, involving complete union and absorption in the divine. It's about merging your consciousness with the Divine Mother.

These paths are not meant to be followed in a specific order, and individuals may find themselves drawn to different ones at different stages of their spiritual journey. Ultimately, all paths lead to the same goal: Connection with the Divine.

ABOUT THE AUTHOR

Deepika, the author of this book, holds a professional qualification in **Company Secretaryship** (CS) alongside degrees in **Master of Commerce** in Business Policy and Corporate Governance (M.Com (BP & CG)) and **Law** (LL.B). Driven by a deep interest in spirituality. She enjoys reading, writing, and spending time immersed in nature. She loves to spend time with children.

The author believes this book offers valuable guidance without being preachy, aiming to reach and empower millions. Her commitment to helping others is further evidenced by her studies and practice of alternative healing modalities, including Chakra Meditation, Emotional Freedom Technique (EFT) and Ho'oponopono.

Should you have any questions, please free to contact her at **cs.deepikadhamija@gmail.com**

GRATITUDE NOTE

To My Wonderful Readers,

I'm overwhelmed with gratitude for each of you who dived into my book. Your time and interest fuel my passion, and I'm truly honored you chose my words as companions.

Writing a book is a shared adventure, and it wouldn't be possible without a community of readers like you. Thank you for being part of this journey that brings stories to life.

I poured my heart into these pages, hoping the ideas and insights would spark something meaningful for you. Whether you found practical advice, a touch of inspiration, or simply something to ponder, that would make me incredibly happy. Feel free to share your thoughts and reviews. You can also connect with me through e-mail at **cs.deepikadhamija@gmail.com**

Once again, thank you from the deepest part of my heart. Your support means the world, and I sincerely hope my words left a positive mark on your life.

With deepest appreciation,
Deepika

www.ingramcontent.com/pod-product-compliance
Lightning Source LLC
Chambersburg PA
CBHW031146130726
47988CB00006B/2558